ZBRUSH USER GUIDE

YOUR SIMPLIFIED MANUAL TO MASTERING THE ART OF DIGITAL SCULPTING

ISAAC LEMMINGS

LEGAL NOTICE

TABLE OF CONTENT

LEGAL NOTICE II

TABLE OF CONTENT III

INTRODUCTION XV

New Features in the Latest ZBrush Software XVI

    Mask Region... xvi

    ZRemesher 4.0... xvi

    Slime Bridge xvi

    Dynamic Symmetry xvi

    UV Map: Unwrap xvii

    Redshift xvii

OVERVIEW OF THIS BOOK XVII

CHAPTER 1 1

EXPLORING ZBRUSH INTERFACE 1

Introduction to Pixologic ZBrush 1

Staring ZBrush 1

MacOSX and Windows Versions.. 2

System Requirements.. 2

3D Applications Supported 4

Installation 5

Activation.. 8

    Online Activation... 8

    Offline Activation 9

    Changing from Online to Offline Activation 9

Uninstalling ZBrush 11

Exploring the ZBrush Interface 11

    Title Bar 11

    QuickSave.. 11

    See-through.. 12

    Unlock 12

    Hide/Restore/Close 12

    Canvas Document 12

    Palettes 12

One Open Subpalette 13

    Palette Popup 14

    SubPalette Popup 14

    Trays 14

    Shelves.. 14

Opening and Saving a ZTool and ZBrush Document 14

    Note.. 15

QuickSave and AutoSave 15

Hot Keys... 16

    Custom HotKey Settings 16

Mouse Wheel Support.. 16

    Assigning a Palette to a HotKey 16

Assigning a Brush to a Hotkey..17
Saving Your Hotkeys..17
Loading Hotkeys..17
Restore Default Hotkeys..17
SELF-EVALUATION TEST 18

CHAPTER 2 19

SCULPTING BRUSHES 19

INTRODUCTION..19
SCULPTING BRUSHES 19
CATEGORIES OF BRUSH 19
Smooth Brushes..19
Several Smooth Brushes 19
Select a Smooth brush of your Choice 20
Smooth Brush Modes..20
WEIGHT STRENGTH 21
Clip Brushes 22
Selecting and using Clip Brushes 22
CURVE BRUSHES 23
Curve 23
Curve Mesh...23
Curve Mesh Insert 23
Curve Surface 24
Move Curve 24
PLANAR, TRIM, AND POLISH BRUSHES 24
Planar brushes..24
Trim brushes...26
Polish brushes...26
Groom Brushes..26
Groom Hairtoss 26
Groomer Strong...26
Groom Clumps 27
Groom Fast Lengthen 27
Groom Root Colorize 27
Groomer Magnet 27
Groomer Twist...27
Groom Twist Slow 27
Groom Spike 27
Groom Spin Knot 27
Pen brushes 27
Insert Mesh Brush 28
Curve Bridge Brush..29
Creating a bridge...30
BRIDGE CONSTRAINTS...32
ZSKETCH BRUSHES 32
Armature 32
Sketch 1, 2 and 3 32
Smooth 1, 2, 3 and 4 33

The Smooth 1, 2, 3 and 4 Brushes 33
FLUSH...33
FlushDynamic 34
FlushResize 34
BULGE 34
Bulge & Flush 34
PUSHPULL...34
Fuse 34
ALPHA 3D VECTOR DISPLACEMENT MESHES 34
Standard..35
Move 35
Inflat 35
Elastic 36
Displace 36
Magnify 36
Blob 36
Pinch...36
Flatten 37
Clay...37
Morph...37
Layer...38
Nudge..38
SNAKE HOOK...38
SELF-EVALUATION TEST 38

CHAPTER 3 ....**39**

INTRODUCTION TO DIGITAL SCULPTING **39**

INTRODUCTION...39
DIGITAL SCULPTING...39
USE OF SYMMETRY IN DIGITAL SCULPTING...40
Symmetry across an Axis...41
Poseable Symmetry 41
Note..43
RADIAL SYMMETRY 44
USE OF ALPHA IN DIGITAL SCULPTING..44
Using Alphas...45
Obtaining Alphas 45
TOOL PALETTE..46
Copy Tool..46
Paste Tool...46
Import...46
Export 46
Clone 46
MAKE POLYMESH3D 46
Sub-tool 47
Geometry 48
Masking...49
Projection Master..50

v

Using Projection Master..*50*
PIXOL TO POLYGON RATIO *51*
Controls *51*
Colors Option...*52*
Material Option *52*
Fade Option *52*
EFFECTS OF FADE ON TEXTURING *52*
Deformation Option *52*
Normalize Option *53*
ARRAY MESH *53*
Array Mesh Stages...*54*
Array Mesh and Nano Mesh *54*
Duplicating a NanoMesh with an ArrayMesh *54*
Converting an Array Mesh to a NanoMesh *55*
ARRAYMESH PRESETS..*56*
ArrayMesh Settings...*56*
Transpose *56*
LOCK POSITION, LOCK SIZE *57*
TRANSFORM STAGE...*57*
Append New *58*
Insert New *58*
Reset..*58*
Delete *58*
Copy, Paste..*58*
Repeat *58*
Chain *58*
Offset...*59*
Scale *59*
Pivot *59*
Extrude *59*
TUTORIAL *60*
SELF-EVALUATION TEST *60*

CHAPTER 4 ....**61**

SUBTOOLS AND FIBERMESH **61**

INTRODUCTION TO SUBTOOLS IN ZBRUSH *61*
SUBTOOL SUBPALETTE...*61*
Visibility Sets *61*
List All *62*
New Folder *62*
ARROW BUTTONS...*62*
Up arrow *62*
Down arrow...*62*
Up and over the arrow *62*
Down and over the arrow *62*
Rename *63*
AUTOREORDER *63*
All Low...*63*

All High *63*
Duplicate *64*
Append *64*
Insert *64*
Delete *65*
Del Other *65*
Del All *65*
Split *66*
Split Hidden *66*
Groups Split *66*
Split to Similar Parts *66*
Split to Parts *66*
Split Unmasked Points *66*
Split Masked Points *66*
Merge *66*
MergeDown *66*
MergeSimilar *67*
Merge Visible *67*
Boolean *67*
BevelPro *68*
Remesh *68*
Remesh All *68*
Res *68*
Polish *68*
PolyGrp *68*
Project *69*
Project All *69*
Dist *69*
Mean *69*
ProjectionShell *69*
Extract *69*
FiberMesh in ZBrush *70*
Tutorial 1 .... *70*
Self-Evaluation Test *71*

CHAPTER 5 .... **72**

ZSPHERES **72**

Introduction... *72*
Display properties... *73*
Density *73*
Color *73*
Size *73*
DSmooth *73*
DRes *73*
Creating Armatures Using ZSpheres *74*
Skinning in ZSpheres *76*
Adaptive Skinning *76*
Unified Skinning *77*

ZSKTECHING 77

ZSKETCH WITH A ZSPHERE STRUCTURE 78

3D SKETCHING ON A SUBTOOL 79

BRUSHES USED IN ZSKTECHING 81

RIGGING USING ZSPHERES..81

   Note...82

SELF-EVALUATION TEST 83

CHAPTER 6 ....**84**

DYNAMESH, NANOMESH, AND ZREMESHER..**84**

INTRODUCTION: DYNAMESH..84

DYNAMESH AREA..84

   DynaMesh 85

   Groups...85

   Polish..85

   Blur 85

   Project 85

   Resolution...85

   Add 86

   Sub..86

CREATE SHELL 86

   Thickness 87

   ZRemesher...87

   FreezeGroup 87

   Keep Groups 88

   Target Polygons Count 88

   Half...88

   Same...88

   Double 88

   Adaptive Size 89

   NanoMesh 89

TUTORIAL..89

MERGING SUBTOOLS..90

SELF-EVALUATION TEST 90

CHAPTER 7 ....**92**

SHADOWBOX..**92**

INTRODUCTION: SHADOWBOX 92

CREATING 3D OBJECTS USING SHADOWBOX 92

MODIFYING 3D OBJECTS IN THE SHADOWBOX 94

   Symmetry in the ShadowBox..95

ATTRIBUTES OF THE SHADOWBOX WITH SUBTOOLS 95

MAKING USE OF REFERENCES ON WORKING PLANES 95

USING ALPHAS IN SHADOWBOX 95

HIDING WORKING PLANES..97

TUTORIAL..98

   Prototyping Models with a Shadowbox 98

   Shadowbox Resolution 98

SELF-EVALUATION TEST 99

CHAPTER 8 ....**100**

MATERIALS IN ZBRUSH **100**

INTRODUCTION: MATERIALS IN ZBRUSH...100
    MatCap Materials *100*
    Standard Materials *100*
    Material Palette *100*
    Load...*101*
    Save...*101*
    LightBox Materials *101*
LIGHTBOX NAVIGATION..102
LIGHTBOX PREFERENCES...102
SAVE AS STARTUP MATERIAL 103
    Show Used...*103*
    CopyMat / PasteMat..*103*
    WaxModfiers...*103*
    Strength..*103*
    Spec *103*
    Fresnel *104*
    Exponent *104*
    Radius...*104*
    Temperature *104*
    Modifiers *104*
COPYSH 105
    PasteSH *105*
    Ambient..*105*
    Diffuse *105*
    Specular..*105*
    Transparency..*105*
    Reflectivity *106*
    Metallicity *106*
    Noise *106*
    Env. Reflection..*106*
APPLY DIFFERENT MATERIALS TO A SUBTOOL 107
SELF-EVALUATION TEST 107

CHAPTER 9 ....**109**

TEXTURING IN ZBRUSH **109**

INTRODUCTION: TEXTURES IN ZBRUSH..109
    Import..*109*
    Export *109*
    Clone *109*
    MakeAlpha *109*
FILLLAYER..109
    Cd *109*
    CropAndFill *109*
    GrabDoc *110*

Texture Palette 110
Spotlight 110
Rotate...110
Scale 111
Opacity 111
BACKGROUND OPACITY...111
Fade..111
QUICK SELECT 112
TILE PROPORTIONAL...112
Tile Selected 112
Tile Unified 112
Front...112
Back..113
Delete 113
Duplicate 113
Union..113
SNAPSHOT 3D..114
Frame 114
FIL H- MIRROR H 114
FLIP V - MIRROR V..115
Extend H...115
Extend V 115
Tile H 116
Tile V...116
Clone 116
Smudge 117
Contrast..117
Saturation...118
Hue 118
Intensity..119
Paint 120
TEXTURING WITH SPOTLIGHT...120
POLYPAINTING 121
TUTORIAL 1 121
Texture maps..121
SELF-EVALUATION TEST 122

CHAPTER 10 123

UV MASTER 123

INTRODUCTION: UV MASTER...123
Unwrap All..123
Symmetry 123
Polygroups..123
USE EXISTING UV SEAMS 124
ENABLE CONTROL PAINTING 124
Protect..125
Attract 125
Erase...126

AttractFromAmbientOCCl 126
    Density 126
    Work On Clone 127
Copy UVs, Paste UVs 128
    Flatten, Unflatten 128
    Check Seams 128
    Clear Maps 129
LoadCtrlMap, and SaveCtrlMap 129
Self-Evaluation Test 129

CHAPTER 11 ....**130**

LIGHTING **130**

Introduction: Light Palette 130
    Load and Save 130
    Light Placement 130
XPos, YPos, and ZPos 131
    Radius 131
    Light Color 131
    Intensity 131
    Ambient 131
    Distance 131
    Background 132
    Zoom 132
    Create 132
Image thumbnail 132
    Exposure 133
    Gamma 133
Longitude and Latitude 133
    Tilt 133
Lightcap 133
    Lightcap preview 133
    NewLight 134
    Del light 134
Lightcap Adjustment 134
    Exposure 134
    Hue 134
    Saturation 134
    Intensity 134
Lightcap Horizon 134
    Horizon Opacity 135
    Color C1 - C4 135
    Horizon Opacity O1 -O4 135
    Rate Top and Rate Bottom 135
    Lights Type 135
    Sun 135
    Point 135
    Spot 135
    Glow 136

Radial 136
Lights Shadow 136
Intensity..136
Shadow Curve 136
Length 136
ZMode 136
Uni 137
Blur 137
Rays 137
Aperture 137
ENVIRONMENT MAPS 137
Gdm - Global Diffuse Map icon 137
Gsm - Global Specular Map icon 138
Gdi - Global Diffuse Intensity...138
Gsi - Global Specular Intensity...138
SELF-EVALUATION TEST 138

CHAPTER 12 139

RENDERING 139

INTRODUCTION: KEYSHOT RENDERER 139
RENDER PALETTE 139
Cursor 139
Render 139
Best..139
Preview..140
Fast..140
Flat 140
EXTERNAL RENDERER 140
KeyShot 140
Max Faces 140
AUTO MERGE MODE...141
GROUP BY MATERIALS 141
SEND DOCUMENT COLOR 142
RENDER PROPERTIES 142
3D POSTERIZE..142
SMOOTH NORMALS 142
MATERIALS BLEND - RADIUS 143
BPR RENDER PASS..143
BPR TRANSPARENCY 144
Strength...144
NFactor..144
ByColor 145
CFactor 145
Refract 145
BPR Shadow 145
FStrength 145
GStrength 145
Rays...146

Angle 146
Res 146
VDepth 146
LDepth 146
Max Dist 147
BPR AO 147
Strength 147
Color 147
Angle 147
Res 147
Gamma 147
BPR SSS 148
SSS Acros Subtools 148
Res 148
Blur 148
BPR Filter 148
F1- F8 148
Filter (default > Noise) 149
BlendMode (default > Add) 149
Strength 149
Mask 149
Shadow 149
AO 149
SSS 150
Int 150
Hue 150
Sat 150
ANTIALIASING 151
Blur 151
Edge 151
SuperSample 151
Depth Cue 151
Fog 152
PREVIEW SHADOWS 153
ObjShadow 153
DeepShadow 153
Length 153
Slope 153
Depth 153
Preview Wax 153
Strength 154
Fresnel 154
Radius 154
Temperature 154
Environment 154
Controls 155
Environment 155
Adjustments 156
Controls 156

ZPlugin Palette 156
    Brush 156
    Brush Increment 156
    Homepage 156
    Decimation Master 156
Self-Evaluation Test 156

CHAPTER 13 ....**158**

DYNAMICS **158**

Introduction to Dynamics 158
Dynamics Palette 158
    Simulation Iterations 158
    Strength 158
    Firmness 158
    On Masked 158
    On Brushed 159
    Fade Border 159
    Self-Collision 159
    Floor Collision 159
    Allow Shrink 159
    Allow Expand 159
    Gravity 159
    Liquify 160
    Set Direction 160
    Gravity Strength 160
    Inflate, Inflate Amount 160
    Deflate, Deflate Amount 160
    Expand, Expand Amount 161
    Contract, Contract Amount 161
    Collision Volume 161
    Recalc 161
    Resolution 161
    Inflate 161
    Run Simulation 161
    Max Simulation Points 162
Self-Evaluation Test 162

CONCLUSION **163**

INDEX **164**

INTRODUCTION

The Pixologic ZBrush is a well-known digital sculpting tool that combines painting, texturing, and 3D and 2.5D modeling. Utilizing a patented Pixol technology, it aids in the saving of information like lighting, material, color, orientation, and depth for each point that comprises every item that is seen on the screen. ZBrush differs from traditional modeling packages in that it focuses more on traditional sculpting, which is a peculiar contrast.

Using ZBrush, several studios—including ILM, Weta Digital, Epic Games, and Electronic Arts—create "high-resolution" models (with more than 40 million polygons) for use in their movies, video games, and animations. Because of ZBrush's dynamic resolution levels, sculptors are empowered to make global or regional changes to their models.

The main feature of ZBrush is its ability to substitute sculpted medium- and high-frequency elements for painted bump maps. The finer elements of the mesh can be applied to a lower poly version of the same model by using the normal maps that you make.

They can also be exported as a displacement map, albeit in this case, a greater resolution is usually required for the lower poly version. The completed 3D model can also be projected onto a background to produce a 2.5D image, which can then be further edited. Following that, work on an alternative 3D model for the same scene may start. This allows users to alter complex landscapes without causing the processing load to increase noticeably.

Pixologic, a company founded by Ofer Alon, created ZBrush. In 1999, the program was showcased at SIGGRAPH. This special software's demo version, 1.55, was made available in 2003, and the 3.1 version was launched in 2007. ZBrush 4 was postponed from its August 2009 release date on the Mac and Windows platforms. September of that year saw the release of ZBrush 3.5, which included new capabilities that had been intended for ZBrush 4.

ZBrush was acquired by the software enterprise Maxon in 2022, a long time after. Since then, ZBrush has been a part of the Maxon One subscription service provided by the corporation. Additionally, the benefit of the strong partnership with Maxon's development team has resulted in the incorporation of the company's Redshift renderer into ZBrush.

New Features in the Latest ZBrush Software

ZBrush is considered the best 3D modeling program available. With a range of customizable brushes, you may mold, texture, and paint digital clay in real-time with its capabilities. ZBrush has become a major force in the art world, adopted by animation firms, video game makers, toy and collectible producers, jewelry designers, vehicle and airplane designers, illustrators, and artists worldwide.

With new capabilities that allow artists to work much more quickly and freely, ZBrush continues down the same road as its predecessors in terms of both creativity and productivity.

With its capacity to work naturally and explore to an acclaimed degree, this version gives artists greater flexibility to showcase their creative ideas and discover a variety of working methods that were previously unimaginable. Prepare to unleash your inner artist!

Mask Region

You can make a mask outline using the Mask area, and ZBrush will fill it in automatically with a single button click. Also, the function is capable of operating in many regions. You can designate sections before filling if you'd want additional control.

ZRemesher 4.0

Updates to ZRemesher have resulted in improved performance and other features. Now that caching has been added, it is feasible to compute a new remesh and alter settings fast. Users can quickly compare different versions by using the Undo History feature, even though only one undo is made.

Slime Bridge

You can be sure that your creature creation will be drooling when you activate this option. It helps conceal two mesh sections and, with a single button press, produces instant drool, melted cheese, or slime. Using this flexible feature, you can also make a variety of organic gooey things.

Dynamic Symmetry

Using the Gizmo's current location as a reference, "Dynamic Symmetry" allows you to determine which symmetry axis to use. As a new addition to Local Symmetry, you may now scale, rotate, and shift the Gizmo location without having to break the symmetry.

UV Map: Unwrap

The UV Map sub-palette has a new section used for the unwrapping of the model. It also brings about the addition of Creases which can be used for the creation of seams hence making it much easier to unwrap models found inside ZBrush.

Redshift

Render directly from ZBrush using the Redshift* renderer. Create stunning renders with the new Redshift materials, which include shadow catchers, metal, glass, reflections, and subsurface scattering. It is important to remember that Redshift needs to be deployed as a standalone application.

OVERVIEW OF THIS BOOK

ZBrush is a one-stop for anyone who likes to edit images or who is inclined to digital sculpting. This book provides all that you need to ensure your images are well-sculpted with the best edit features.

This book has 13 chapters, carefully written with step-by-step illustrations to aid the understanding of steps that seem rather complex.

Below are snippets from each of the chapters in this book;

Chapter 1: Exploring ZBrush Interface

This book's first chapter begins with a brief introduction to the 3D modeling software known as Pixologic ZBrush. In this section, you will discover all you need to know to successfully install and activate the Zbrush program.

You will also become familiar with the interface components that include a title bar, canvas document, palettes, trays, and shelves. You will also gain knowledge on how to open and save documents created with ZTool and ZBrush.

Chapter 2: Sculpting Brushes

What would be the point of sculpting if you couldn't use brushes? This chapter will acquaint you with all of the brushes that you will later encounter in the course of the book. You will acquire knowledge regarding the many types of brushes that are on offer, such as clip brushes, curve brushes, planar and trim brushes, Groom brushes, Pen brushes, ZSketch brushes, and a great deal more.

Chapter 3: Introduction to Digital Sculpting

In this chapter, you will take your first steps towards learning digital sculpting. This chapter will teach you how to employ both symmetry and alpha in digital sculpture. Additionally, you will learn about the array mesh, the projection master, and the tool palette.

Chapter 4: SubTools and FiberMesh

Similar to the tools ZBrush offers, it also offers us a selection of auxiliary tools that can be quite useful throughout the sculpting process. This chapter covers the use of the sub tool and its sub palette, which includes many more options in addition to arrow buttons and functions for renaming, copying, pasting, appending, duplicating, inserting, deleting, and remeshing. You will also be taught how to use ZBrush's fiber mesh in addition to this.

Chapter 5: ZSpheres

This chapter will shed some light on the application of ZSpheres for you. You will learn how to make armatures by utilizing ZSpheres, as well as how to add skin to ZSpheres. In addition, you will learn about ZSketching, which will contain an explanation of the many brushes that may be utilized while working in ZSketching.

Chapter 6: DynaMesh, NanoMesh, and ZRemesher

You will learn about DynaMesh, a feature of ZBrush, in this chapter. Along with it, you will learn about the several palettes beneath it, including groups, polish, blur, project, resolution, and thickness. After learning about the different options available to you within ZRemesher, such as freeze groups, goal polygon count, is half, and the same, you will also be educated about the NanoMesh.

Chapter 7: ShadowBox

This chapter will introduce you to ShadowBox. Here you will learn about the creation of 3D objects with the use of ShadowBox, you will also learn about the modification of 3D objects in ShadowBox. You will also learn about the use of symmetry in ShadowBox and the various attributes of ShadowBox.

Chapter 8: Materials in ZBrush

This chapter discusses the various materials that can be found in ZBrush which are the Matcap and Standard materials. You will also learn about the various materials palette in

ZBrush such as Item info, lightbox materials, CopyMat, PasteMat, Wax Modifiers, etc. You will also learn how to add various materials to an object in ZBrush.

Chapter 9: Texturing in ZBrush

In this chapter, you will learn about the different textures that ZBrush offers, such as Import, Export, Make Alpha, GrabDoc, GrabDocandDepth. You will also learn about the texture palette and the other options that are located under it.

You will also be exposed to Spotlight in this chapter; under the spotlight area, you will discover how to scale, rotate, remove, duplicate, union, and much more.

Chapter 10: UV Master

This chapter will discuss the UV Master in detail including all of the various features under it such as unwrapping, symmetry, polygroups, Protect, Attract, work on a clone, etc.

Chapter 11: Lighting

This chapter discusses Lighting as it pertains to ZBrush. Here you will also learn about the light palette which includes features like light placement, light switches, light color, intensity, ambient, light properties, etc.

Chapter 12: Rendering

In this chapter, you will learn about the KeyShot Renderer. You will also learn about the Render palette and the various features under it such as the cursor, Render, fast, and flat.

Chapter 13: Dynamics

The final chapter in this book covers all the information you require to understand Dynamics. The Dynamics palette and its several features, such as hardness, On Masked, On Brushed, Allow Shrink, Allow Expand, and many more, will also be covered.

It is also important to note that each chapter ends with a self-evaluation test; try to complete theM

CHAPTER 1

EXPLORING ZBRUSH INTERFACE

Introduction to Pixologic ZBrush

ZBrush, a program for digital sculpting and painting, has revolutionized the 3D industry with its powerful capabilities and intuitive interface. ZBrush is one of the most capable applications available to digital artists today, with a slick user interface. ZBrush's vast range of features was created with user convenience in mind, providing an easy and inspiring creative experience. With ZBrush, the only limitation is your creativity due to its infinite polygon count.

The menus in ZBrush have a circular layout and operate in a non-linear, mode-free way. This opens up new possibilities for interactions between 2.5D Pixels, 2D images, and 3D models.

ZBrush gives users the tools they need to quickly conceptualize and create 2D or 3D concepts. ZBrush comes with tools that may be used to create photorealistic renderings that include an environment and lighting. The model's extensive sharing features allow you to rapidly prepare it for 3D printing or use it in any other digital application.

As a result of ZBrush's powerful computational capabilities, users may sculpt and paint with thousands of polygons without having to spend a fortune on expensive graphics gear. This is why ZBrush is used by amateur filmmakers as well as video game developers.

You can now sculpt and paint with the same brushes and tools you've always used without having to worry about technological challenges or steep learning curves.

Staring ZBrush

If you are new to ZBrush and you have just acquired it, I am sure you will be more than excited to see what it is capable of. Just like any other software, you should get to know about certain basic things before you get going.

In this section, you will learn about the various things to do to be fully accustomed to using ZBrush.

1

MacOSX and Windows Versions

Macintosh uses the Cmd(Apple) key, in contrast to Windows, which uses the Ctrl key. Throughout this book, the Ctrl key will be discussed the most, albeit it may also be written as Ctrl/Cmd. It may be easier to use the Cmd key instead of the Ctrl key if you're using a Macintosh; if your keyboard supports both keys, you can use whichever one you like.

The same is true for the Windows Enter key, which is referred to as the Return key on Macintoshes. If you use a Mac, press the Return key whenever you see the Enter key used in this book.

It is also worth mentioning that the Close/Quit, Hide, Minimize, and Maximize buttons can be found at the top right side of the Windows and the top left on the Mac OS X.

System Requirements

Below are the highly recommended settings for the Optimum use of ZBrush in Windows.

- **OS**: 64-bit editions of Windows 10 or 11.

- **CPU**: Intel i7/i9/Xeon technology and newer or the use of AMD Ryzen/Threadripper and newer.

- **RAM**: 16GB needed for working with multi-million poly models. (32 +GB preferred).

- **HDD**: 100 GB of free hard drive space for ZBrush and its scratch disk. However, SSD is highly recommended.

- **Pen Tablet**: Tablet with a pressure-sensing pen, such as those made by Wacom, XPen, XenceLabs, Huion, and so on. (WinTab API compatibility is required.)

- **Monitor**: 1920 x 1080 resolution or higher with a 32-bit color.

- **Video card**: must offer support for OpenGL 3.3 or higher and Vulkan 1.1 or higher.

- **Redshift**: Has earlier stated, it must be installed separately hence it has its system requirement.

Minimum System Requirements

- **OS:** 64-bit editions of Windows 10 or 11. 32 bits systems are no longer supported

- **CPU:** Intel i7/i9 technology and newer or AMD Ryzen and newer.

- **RAM:** 4 GB (however 6+ GB is highly recommended)

- **HDD:** 20 GB of free hard disk for ZBrush and its scratch disk.

- **Pen Tablet:** Pointer device or suitable pressure-sensitive tablet. (WinTab API compatibility is required.)

- **Monitor:** 1280 x 1024 monitor resolution with 32-bit color.

- **Video card:** Must offer support for OpenGL 3.3 or higher and Vulkan 1.1 or higher.

- **Redshift:** Redshift has also said earlier that it has its requirements.

For Macintosh; I highly recommended

- **OS:** Mac OS: 10.14 or above.

- **CPU:** Apple Silicon technology.

- **RAM:** 16 GB is required for working with multi-million polys. (32 +GB preferred).

- **HDD:** 100GB of free hard drive space ZBrush along with its scratch disk. (SSD drive highly recommended.)

- **Pen Tablet:** Mouse or compatible pressure-sensitive tablet.

- **Monitor:** 1920 x 1080 resolution or higher with millions of colors.

- **Video card:** must offer support for OpenGL 3.3 or higher.

- **Redshift:** this must have its unique system requirements.

Minimum System Requirements

- **OS:** Mac OS: 10.14 or above.

- **CPU:** Intel i7/ i9 technology or above.

- **RAM:** 4 GB (6+ GB highly recommended)

- **HDD:** 20 GB of free hard drive space for ZBrush and its scratch disk.

- **Pen Tablet:** Mouse or compatible pressure-sensitive tablet.

- **Monitor:** 1280 x 1024 resolutions with millions of colors.

- **Video card:** Must provide support for OpenGL 3.3 or higher.

- **Redshift:** this has its unique system requirements.

Redshift Requirements

- **Microsoft Windows:** 64-bit Windows 10

- **Linux:** 64-bit distribution with the use of glibc 2.17 or later.

- **Apple macOS:** Big Sur (11.5) via Monterey (12.5) and macOS 13 Ventura.

3D Applications Supported

- **Autodesk Maya (Windows, Linux, macOS):** 64-bit edition. 2016.5 Or later.

- **Autodesk 3ds Max (Windows):** 64-bit edition. 2015 or later.

- **Maxon Cinema 4D (Windows and macOS):** 64-bit edition. R21 or later.

- **Maxon Cinema 4D (Linux Command Line):** 64-bit edition. R21 or later.

- **Side FX Houdini (Windows, Linux):** 64-bit edition. 17.5 Or later.

- **SideFX Houdini (macOS):** 64-bit edition. 18.0 or later

- **Foundry Katana (Windows, Linux):** 64-bit edition. 3.0v1 or later.

- **Blender (Windows, Linux):** 64-bit edition. 2.83LTS or later

Minimum Requirements

- 8 GB of RAM

- Processor with SSE2 support (Pentium 4 or better)

- **For Windows and Linux:** NVIDIA GPU with CUDA compute capability 5.0 or higher and 8 GB VRAM.

- **For macOS:** Apple M1 16 GB or AMD "Navi" or "Vega" GPU or later with 8 GB VRAM or more.

- Single GPU

Recommended Requirements

- 16 GB of RAM or more.

- Core i7 or Xeon equivalent, 3.0GHz or higher.

- For both Windows and Linux, you'll need an NVIDIA graphics processing unit (GPU) with CUDA compute capability 7.0 or above and 8 GB of video memory (VRAM). For hardware-accelerated ray tracing, we advise using an NVIDIA Quadro, Titan, or GeForce RTX GPU.

- Any AMD "Navi" or "Vega" GPU or later, with 8 GB VRAM or more, or an Apple M1 with 16 GB of RAM are all suitable options for macOS.

- Multiple GPUs.

Installation

Please follow the steps below to configure ZBrush on your device. Whether you're updating an existing installation or installing ZBrush for the first time, these guidelines still apply.

Windows

To open the ZBrush installer,

- Double-click **the file you downloaded**. It could take a few moments for the installer to unpack itself into memory and move on to the next screen. Kindly wait. A UAC (User Account Control) alert will also appear.

- To proceed, please **select Yes**.

MacOS

- Simply **double-click the downloaded DMG file** to begin mounting. This usually opens the installer application in a new tab or window. If the ZBrush installer

5

doesn't open automatically, you can find it in the Devices folder of your Finder window. From that location, you may find the software installation.

- To run the installer, simply **double-click the icon**. The installer will now unpack itself into memory and **proceed to the next screen**, which could take a minute or two. If you're using Mac OS X, you'll be prompted to enter your username and password.

Installing software typically begins with the installer asking the user to select their preferred language. ZBrush itself will be localized to this language by default as well.

- Choose **the language you like from the drop-down menu**, and then click **OK** to begin the installation.

Next, make sure you go over the ZBrush End User License Agreement very carefully. After installing ZBrush, you agree to all of the terms and restrictions about its use. Be aware that this contract has legal force behind it. If you refuse to give your permission, the installation will be canceled. So, by installing and using ZBrush, you implicitly agree to the terms and conditions of the EULA.

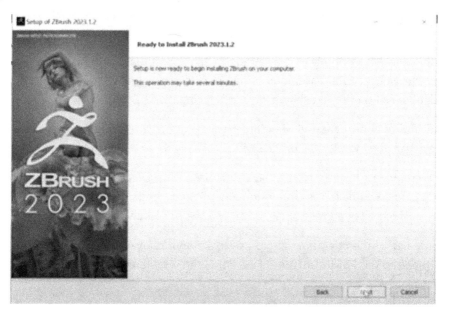

When you are done with the above; you can then proceed to make your choice of the path of installation;

6

The default path where ZBrush should be installed will be indicated by the installation. ZBrush will be installed on Windows under the C:| Program Files | Pixologic directory. On macOS, it will be placed in the Applications folder.

- If the suggested site is fine, proceed by clicking the **"Next" button**.

- Choose **the yellow folder icon** if you'd like to change where ZBrush is installed. This will open a file browser where you can locate the installation folder on your hard disk.

- Click the **"Next" button** when you're ready to move forward.

It is up to you to decide which components to install. While ZBrush will undoubtedly be installed, you have the option to not install any official-looking plugins or the program's documentation. Although installing every component and leaving everything checked is advised, you are free to uncheck any components that you would rather not install.

- **Click the "Next" button when you're ready to move forward.**

Please keep in mind that setting things up is strongly recommended. Restarting the installer will allow you to add any components you skipped but later decided you wanted. You can add or remove features and modify your current ZBrush installation by doing this.

Everything installs smoothly as it always does. Remember that installing software can take some time, which could make your computer sluggish or unresponsive. It is essential to concentrate just on the installation while it is taking place.

A slideshow of photos created with ZBrush will be displayed throughout this period. After a little pause, the installer will proceed automatically to the following screen.

After finishing, the installer will display a final page with several options for what happens when it shuts. You have the option to launch ZBrush itself, open ZClassroom to view a variety of video tutorials for ZBrush, or browse the documentation.

With the use of the checkboxes, you can make your choice of items you would like to open then tap the **Finish button.** Once done, the installer will close and any items you have chosen will be opened.

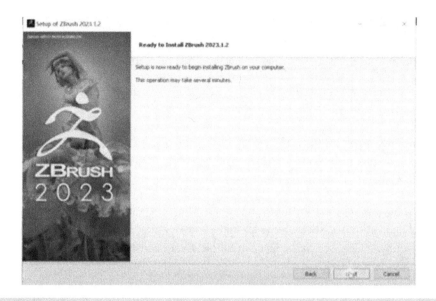

Activation

When you initially start ZBrush, an activation box will pop up, giving you the following choices:

You have the option of activating online in a matter of minutes after logging in with your Pixologic ID or performing the necessary steps offline.

Details on both decisions are provided below.

Online Activation

The most popular and greatest option is this one. It allows ZBrush to be activated in a matter of minutes, so you can start using the program right away. It is recommended that you make use of this option if your device is internet-connected or if you can establish a temporary online connection. Please be aware that to activate online, you must be aware of your Pixologic ID. Enter the password and email address you used to establish your Pixologic ID.

- To view your entered password, select **the eye icon**. Then, simply go where it says **"Login."**

You will be prompted with a screen listing the licenses you currently have active along with the total number of activations for each when you run your preferred web browser. For the great majority of users, only one license will be displayed.

- To activate a license, just click the **Select button** to the right of your preferred license.

After finishing, a description of the computer being used for license activation will be requested on the next page. Additionally, the default will match the name that the operating system you are using has already assigned to the computer.

This activation will appear in the future under whatever you type into My Licenses here. Give each activation a distinct name so that you can quickly identify between them when viewing your My Licenses page, as each Single-User license can have two activations (or more with Volume licensing).

Instead of using a general term like "Workstation," please provide a more accurate, machine-specific description.

Offline Activation

If your computer won't load the activation website or doesn't have internet access, you can use offline activation. This is a slightly more complicated process than online activation, but it's still quite simple.

It's simple to carry out. The Request file that ZBrush creates can be saved to any internet-connected device. Once you follow the instructions on that page, ZBrush will provide you with an Activation File to import.

Changing from Online to Offline Activation

At the lower part of the right of the Pixologic ID window in ZBrush,

- Select **the button for Offline Activation**.

A new window will appear with details on ZBrush. The URL is https://pixologic.com/offline/; please read it and write it down or make a note of it elsewhere. You will require an internet-connected computer to view that website.

After you confirm the activation, ZBrush will ask you to save a "Request File" with a name like "request ZBrush2018 activation. zreq". It is advised that you store this data on a USB flash drive or other portable device.

After completing the aforementioned procedure, you can take the portable media containing the Request File to any internet-connected computer. Go to the https://pixologic.com/offline/ webpage after opening a web browser.

This page will request your Pixologic ID,

- Select the **Choose File button** to browse and choose **the Request File** from your portable media then choose **the Start activation button**.

Once then you will be directed to a page that shows your account license and the seats available for each of them.

- Simply choose **the Select button** close to the license you would like to make use of. Most users will have just one license shown.

On the following screen, you will be asked for some information about the device that the license is being activated on. Your operating system will assign a default name to your computer.

This activation will appear under whatever you type in My Licenses in the future. You can have two activations per Single-User license (or more with Volume licensing), thus it's useful to give each one a different name so you can quickly identify them while looking through your My Licenses page.

Instead of using a general term like "Workstation," please provide a more accurate, machine-specific description.

Once done, you will get a congratulatory message about the activation. You can

- Click **on the download link and save the Activation File**. Once done you can return to the computer where ZBrush has to be activated.

ZBrush may be activated offline, and it will remember that you did so the next time it runs. either imports the activation file you created in the previous step, or aborts the offline activation in progress, returning you to the main Pixologic ID login screen.

- Choose **the. zact file** you've been keeping on your flash drive by clicking the **"Import Activation File" button**.

The following message appears once ZBrush has finished activating itself after you load the file:

"ZBrush will start normally after you select **OK**, and you may begin working immediately."

Uninstalling ZBrush

For any reason, you might one day need to completely remove ZBrush from your computer.

- Web Deactivation can be accessed via the ZPlugin menu; from there, the license deactivation process can be carried out as described above. If you don't deactivate before removing the program from a system, that machine will still be counted against your serial number, which would prohibit you from reactivating the program.

- You can use the Windows Control Panel uninstall tool on Windows and follow the directions. All you need to do on Mac OS X is drag the Users/Public/Pixologic and ZBrush folders to the trash.

- Check the ZBrush installation folder in case any leftover files from the installation procedure were not deleted. Those folders can be deleted if you don't intend to use ZBrush on this machine in the future.

Exploring the ZBrush Interface

Title Bar

The Title Bar is located at the top of the user interface. There you can see statistics and ZBrush's current memory usage. It will be followed immediately by links to many palettes, or menus. When a menu is selected, the palette is displayed.

The NoteBar is located beneath the menus. This displays details on the current user's action. In essence, if Transpose is being utilized as a measuring device, this is helpful.

A variety of interface controls and QuickSave buttons may be found on the right side of the Title Bar.

QuickSave

If you want to save the current Project as a QuickSave file immediately, just press the QuickSave button. There is no need to select a filename or wait for the saving to complete. With the use of the Lightbox's Quicksave tab, you'll be able to access and reload your QuickSave files.

11

See-through

To change the ZBrush interface's overall transparency, adjust the slider. If you need to quickly work from reference material that is open in a different program, such as a Web browser, this is quite helpful.

Unlock

If peradventure a zscript or plugin gets the interface locked,

- Tap **this button** to have it unlocked.

Hide/Restore/Close

The standard program buttons for concealing or restoring the ZBrush window and also having the program closed.

Canvas Document

Unlike traditional 3D modeling software, ZBrush employs a 2.5D canvas document on which 3D models can be sketched. ZBrush lacks a true 3D space, therefore many of its most prominent and potent features are only accessible through its depth-enabled canvas.

The Zoom controls work on the canvas and enlarges the pixels. They are found in the Document palette. As a result, if you enlarge the image too much, you will begin to see individual pixels, which will reduce its significance. This is similar to enlarging a photograph in a photo editor.

When in Edit mode, you cannot enlarge a 3D model using the canvas zoom. Use Scale to alter the object's size instead. You may maintain clarity while focusing on little details by changing the object's scale. Please remember that scaling does not change the size of your item; rather, it just adjusts the percentage of the canvas that it takes up.

Palettes

All of the materials, including user-created ones, are displayed in the Materials Quick Palette.

If you go to the Material Palette and find the big thumbnail for the Current Material there,

- Choosing **it will open the quick palette**. As an alternative, you can also choose to take the mouse off the canvas and hit F6 (Windows only). The Materials Quick Palette offers various buttons that can be used to work with materials.

- Choose **the name of a palette** to display the palette. Note that Palettes are usually arranged for specific ZBrush features.

ZBrush attempts to maintain the Left and Right Tray palettes visible while the Auto Collapse option is enabled. Palettes close to a recently extended palette could collapse to create space for it.

All palettes will stay open until you click on their title bars if this option is disabled. A double-arrow cursor that appears as you slide the tray panels up or down allows you to access the palettes.

One Open Subpalette

With the use of the One Open Subpalette, any sub-palette that is opened will be closed whenever a new one is opened.

This can be of immense advantage with the navigation of the palette by the reduction of up and down scrolling.

- However, when **the shift button** is held while also clicking **the name of a sub-palette**, all other palettes will be opened.

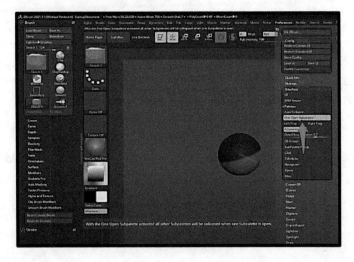

- You can choose **to turn this feature off** to ensure sub-palettes remain open until they are closed.

Palette Popup

Similar options are always available to palettes when they are docked in the left or right trays. There will only be one palette visible in the tray when the Palette Pop-up is enabled. The palette's name will display an alphabetically ordered list of palettes upon clicking, giving the user the option to choose an alternative palette

SubPalette Popup

When this option is switched on, just one sub-palette will be displayed at a time. When the sub-palette is chosen, a list of all the sub-palettes in alphabetical order will be displayed such that other sub-palettes can be chosen.

Trays

You can only have one open palette in the Left Tray at a time if you pick the Left Tray Auto Collapse button. When a new palette expands, the other palettes will instantly shrink in size.

One palette can only be open at a time in the Right Tray when the Auto Collapse button is used. Opening a new palette will cause the others to collapse.

Shelves

Shelves can be arranged in any pattern around the canvas and are movable partitions. Saying "The AAHalf button is on the right shelf" is one example. "The AAHalf button is on the shelf" would also be accurate, even though it is customary to refer to the entire set of four walls at once. A huge object will cause the side of the shelf to automatically extend to fit on that side of the canvas. Objects can be arranged vertically (for the top and bottom shelves) or next to one another for the left and right shelves. It is forbidden for you to shelve menus or submenus. This area is designated for particular user interface elements.

Opening and Saving a ZTool and ZBrush Document

Whenever you are working, you will surely need to save your work. This is when it becomes important to know the difference between 3D models and canvas documents. Because the document can only include 2.5D pixels, it lacks the full 3D data of a model. This means that if you happen to be working on a 3D model and save the document, just a PXO version of the model in its current perspective will be saved. If you wish to keep sculpting in the future, you should use the Tool palette to save your 3D model instead of doing this.

In summary;

- Saving the document will keep the canvas 2.5D content alone. This can be used for illustrations.

- Saving the ZTool will also save the chosen 3D object which includes all of its sub-tools, subdivisions, settings, 3D layers, etc. This applies to models.

- Saving a Project will also save various ZTools all at once. It gives rise to a much bigger file size hence it is not a viable choice for saving various versions of a single ZTool.

Note

Please make it a habit to save frequently and modestly. ZBrush is a program that taxes your computer and utilizes a lot of data. A computer might experience serious issues, such as corrupted files that cannot be restored, with just a small mistake. If you regularly create backups of your work, you will protect yourself from suffering large losses in the unlikely case that something unbelievable occurs. Ascertain that every duplicate has a distinct name, and keep at least three copies in case one gets corrupted. To store your work, you should not rely just on ZBrush's automatic save feature (more on that in a bit).

QuickSave and AutoSave

The AutoSave feature aids in the safeguarding of your work by ensuring it automatically saves a Project periodically or anytime ZBrush gets to an idle state. If ZBrush gets shut down for just about any reason you will be able to bring back your work by loading the temporary file designed by ZBrush.

Under the Options menu, you can determine the maximum amount of time that can pass between saves. ZBrush will keep an eye on what you're doing to avoid interrupting your workflow.

Since the AutoSave feature only works with a dedicated project, it won't overwrite any existing copies of your project. The version that is automatically stored will remain completely separate from any copies that are manually saved. A warning message will be sent to the user informing them to make room on their hard drive if ZBrush does not have enough disk space to save a Tool or Project. Until there is enough room on the screen to save the file, this warning will be visible.

Hot Keys

A "hotkey" is a key or set of keys that, when depressed simultaneously, accelerates the performance of a job (like opening an application) in comparison to the usage of a mouse or other input device. Key combinations or single keys can be used as hotkeys. There are situations where "hotkeys" and "shortcut keys" are used synonymously. Hotkeys can be used with a wide range of operating systems and applications.

Custom HotKey Settings

- Tap and hold **CTRL + ALT** then **click anywhere on the interface item** you would like to assign a hotkey to. This can either be a button, a palette, or a slider.

- Touch **the key on your keyboard** you would like to assign the interface item to or touch ESC to leave.

Mouse Wheel Support

For devices with a mouse wheel, ZBrush 4R5 comes with support for it. The actions that are performed by moving the mouse wheel up or down can be redistributed to other ZBrush sliders, such as the Draw Size slider. To use this function, you must assign a hotkey in the standard way, but you will need to scroll the mouse wheel in place of entering a key command.

Assigning a Palette to a HotKey

- Press and hold **CTRL + ALT > select the Palette**.

- Tap the key on your keyboard you would like to add the interface item to or tap the **ESC to leave**.

The top center of the palette will move to where your cursor is when you press a hotkey that has been assigned to that palette. If the palette cannot be seen in its entirety within the interface, it will be moved upwards in a vertical direction until it fits inside the ZBrush window.

The palettes for Texture and Material as well as Alpha, Stroke, Tools, and Brushes are automatically opened by pressing the keys F1 through F6.

Assigning a Brush to a Hotkey

If you would like to add a brush to a key, follow the set of steps below;

- Press and hold **CTRL + ALT** and select **the brush in the Brush palette**. You can also select a brush icon in the Brush palette or the Brush pop-up.

- Tap **the key on your keyboard** if you would like to assign the interface item to touch ESC to leave.

You also have the option to modify the letter that is used as the last letter of the hotkey that is used to select a brush from the brush popup.

For example, you may change the default combination of B+S+T for the Standard Brush to B+S+X:

- Press **B for the brush popup to be displayed**.

- Touch **the initial letter of the Brush** you would like to make use of.

- Tap **Ctrl + Alt** and select the brush icon in the popup.

- Touch **the key on your keyboard** you would like to make use of.

Saving Your Hotkeys

If you would like to store your hotkeys so that you can always get to use them anytime, **Preferences > Hotkeys > Store**.

You can also choose to store the hotkeys in case you need to always get them assigned. To save your hotkeys press **Preference > Hotkeys > Save**

Loading Hotkeys

If you would like to load your hotkeys, tap **Preferences > Hotkeys > Load.**

Restore Default Hotkeys

If you would like to restore your hotkeys to the initial hotkey setup of ZBrush;

- Press **Preferences > Hotkeys > Restore**.

You can designate any slider to be controlled by moving the mouse wheel up or down in place of a hotkey. Just assign the hotkey as usual, but scroll the mouse wheel in place of tapping a key. This will result in the same outcome.

Self-Evaluation Test

1. Locate the very important aspects of the ZBrush interface such as the Title bar, Canvas, Palettes, Trays, and also the Shelve.

2. Open a ZTool and ZBrush document.

3. Highlight the Hotkeys in ZBrush.

CHAPTER 2

SCULPTING BRUSHES

Introduction

You have access to a large selection of brushes in ZBrush as sculpting tools. All brushes are unique and have a quality that makes them stand out from the others and allows them to do a task that the other brushes cannot. Additionally, several important parameters like Gravity, Wrap Mode, and Density can be used to customize brushes in ZBrush. By altering the settings and storing the brush, you can create personalized copies of any brush that you can use later.

Sculpting Brushes

In this section, you will learn about the main categories of the brush as well as the various brush types that can be found in ZBrush.

Categories of Brush

Smooth Brushes

By averaging the vertices' displacements concerning their neighbors, the Smooth brush can be used to smooth out a surface. This implies that the subdivision level of the model heavily influences the scale across which smoothing takes place. Larger features would be smoothed at a lower subdivision level, while pores in the skin and other minute details would be smoothed at a higher level.

Using Smooth at different subdivision levels allows you to have a great deal of control over how your model behaves. For instance, you could decide to soften a mountain range while preserving all of the intricate details that have been carved in, such as waterways or rugged terrain.

Several Smooth brushes

Smooth brushes come in multiple varieties, each with a distinct set of functions. While some brushes, like Smooth Peaks and Smooth Valleys, use cavity masking to smooth only the interior of a cavity or the tops of the peaks of the geometry, others, like Smooth Valance, Smooth Subdivision, and Smooth Groups, will smooth following the topology of your model.

19

Select a Smooth brush of your Choice

The new Smoothing brush that is activated when you press the Shift key is automatically defined when you select a Smooth brush. Smooth brushes can no longer be selected individually as you could with some other brushes.

Should you need to alter types, use a different Smooth brush.

After that, whenever you press the Shift key, your selection will become active until you switch to a new Smooth brush.

- With the **Shift key held down**, you can alter the parameters of the selected Smooth brush. (Hold **Shift and tweak the Z Intensity slider**, for instance.) The Smooth brush is the only one that will be modified in this way.

Smooth Brush Modes

Smooth Brush Modifiers > Weighted Smooth Mode is a new option in the Brush Palette that modifies the way a smooth brush interacts with the surface.

The smooth brush now has seven distinct modes, each with its own associated Weight Strength slider.

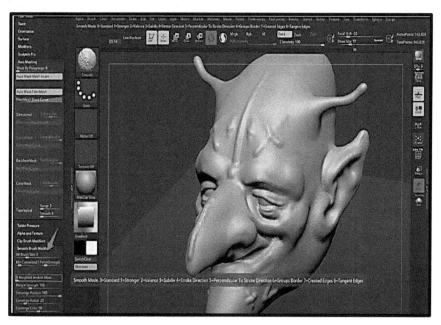

- **0 standards**: this mode will ensure the smooth brush is kept at default.

- **1 Stronger**: this mode will help with the increment of the smooth brush to interact with the surface faster.

- **2 Valance**: When a large number of polygons in the mesh come together at a single location, this option will give that point extra weight. A point that has five faces sharing it, for instance, will have a higher smoothing weight than a point that just has three faces sharing it.

- **3 Subdiv**: this mode helps with the smoothing of the mesh with the same algorithm that is executed when you subdivide a mesh in ZBrush.

- **4 Stroke Direction**: Additionally, this mode will aid in the mesh's smoothing along the stroke's only direction. It's a beautiful way to soften your last stroke while maintaining a lot of the surface detail.

- **5 Perpendicular to Stroke Direction**: this mode smooths the surface detail that is perpendicular to your brush stroke.

- **6 Groups Border**: this mode helps to smooth the mesh but it will also respect the borders of the groups to maintain the line along the border.

- **7 Creased Edges**: this mode will keep the creased edge when smoothed out.

Weight Strength

This parameter allows you to change how sensitive the smooth algorithm is to the surface in each mode. At smaller numbers, the smooth stroke has less of an effect. This slider solely affects the settings for Groups Boundaries and Creased Edges. Numerous additional Smooth brushes are now available, each with a distinct set of skills. The Smooth Peaks and Smooth Valley brushes use cavity masking to smooth only the interior of a cavity or the tops of the peaks of the geometry, while the Smooth Valance, Smooth Subdivision, and Smooth Groups brushes, among others, will execute a smooth depending on the topology of your model.

- Pressing the **Shift key** will bring up the **Smooth Brush icon** and name in the **Brush panel**, in case you've forgotten which Smooth Brush is assigned to **Shift**.

21

Clip Brushes

Clip Brushes are different from other brushes in that they always draw perpendicular to the canvas. Similar to how the Eraser tool removes canvas pixels, you may use these brushes to erase portions of your model and trim off its corners. These Clip brushes just move polygons in the direction of the brush stroke; they don't change the structure of your model.

Since the clip Brushes employ both open and closed curves, it is imperative to know which side the clipped polygons will be pushed to. This causes a shadow to be projected on one side of the curves, pushing any polygon drawn adjacent to them in that direction.

- You may tell ZBrush to move the polygons oppositely by using the **ALT key** after you've made a mistake when drawing a stroke.

The clip brushes treat masking with deference. All you have to do is paint a mask over the area that has to be protected from pushing. Additionally, make sure to inspect your model for any unprotected places because the clip brushes work across the entire depth of the model concerning the curve.

- A curved line can be drawn once by touching **the ALT key with the ClipCurve brush**, and the line's direction can be altered by tapping **the ALT key again**. When using the **ClipCurve brush**, a sharp angle will be created rather than a smooth one if you **double-tap the ALT key**.

- If you hold down the **ALT key** while drawing a circle or rectangle with the **Circle Clip brush**, **ZBrush** will remove all of the mesh inside the shape. If you **hold ALT** and move **the cross indication** over any section of the mesh, the geometry will be pushed outwards.

All of the clip brushes operate in the same way; the only difference between them is their Stroke type.

Selecting and using Clip Brushes

Just like the use of Smooth brushes, Clip brushes can be activated with the use of the hotkey. When choosing a Clip brush in the Brush palette, it will be assigned to a particular hotkey automatically; **Ctrl + Shift**.

When you are making use of a normal brush,

- Tap **Ctrl + Shift** to activate the chosen **Clip brush**. Revert to using the standard brush by letting go of the Ctrl + Shift. You don't have to switch the active normal brush when you select a different Clip brush; the previous brush will be replaced.

Curve Brushes

Curve

This brush makes use of the **newstroke > Curves functions** with the combination of standard sculpting brush. With this, it will be quite possible to sweep your sculpting along a specific curve.

Curve Mesh

Builds a curving path with a cylinder placed down it, the base of which is in line with the working plane of the canvas. Working with a DynaMesh will maximize the benefits of this brush, even though subdivision levels are not supported.

Curve Mesh Insert

Similar to Curve Mesh, with the exception that the curve snaps to the model's surface rather than the canvas plane. Using this brush will prevent subdivision levels from existing in your model.

Within the **Brush > Modifiers sub-palette** the Brush Modifier slider will dominate the number of faces the mesh has when drawn to a model. For instance, the default value of 20 designs a smooth cylinder but if you choose to modify the Brush Modifier to 4 then the mesh will obtain a square cross-section whenever it is drawn.

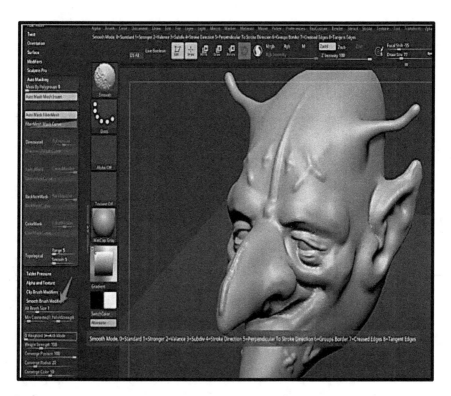

Curve Surface

Similar to the Curve Mesh except for the fact that it inserts a cube along the curve which ends up in the creation of a type of extrusion. Just like other mesh insertion brushes, your model won't have subdivision levels when making use of the brush.

Move Curve

This helps with the combination of the effects of the Curve and also Move brushes for a constant displacement of geometry along the curve path.

Planar, Trim, and Polish Brushes

Planar brushes

You can flatten your model with planar brushes without adding any overlapping geometry. Using one of these brushes, click inside a cavity and drag in that direction to flatten any geometry that is above the click depth. Because the pointer will already be at the highest point of the model, nothing will be flattened when you click on a peak's summit.

- Adjust the thickness of your planar brush strokes with the Imbed slider found in the **Brush > Depth menu.**

Under the Brush tab in Lightbox, under the Planar folder, is where you'll find the Planar Cut brush. It slices a plane at the tilt and depth that you specify at the start of the stroke.

By altering the Embed value in the Brush Depth submenu or by repeatedly clicking the cursor's start, you can increase the depth. The plane will extend as you work outward.

The Planar Cut and Planar brushes work well together. The general plane's angle and depth are first established using Planar Cut, and the details are subsequently filled in using Planar Brush. When you move to the planar brush, control is better than when using the Planar Cut alone.

Trim brushes

Although trim brushes are based on planar brushes, they can behave differently depending on whether the surface of the screen working plane is normal. Unlike planar brushes, which are limited to a chosen area of the surface or a predetermined path, trim brushes are not subject to these custom constraints.

With the help of these brushes, you will be able to freehand sculpt hard surfaces.

Polish brushes

With the use of the polish brush, you can smoothen, flatten, and also shine the surface such that it looks like polished metal.

Groom Brushes

With the FiberMesh tool, grooming brushes are included. These are specialized tools made for FiberMesh model shaping.

These tools are modeled like traditional sculpting brushes; however, their behavior has been adjusted to avoid undesirable results when Fibers are used with them.

Groom Hairtoss

This is a standard grooming brush that is very useful when having to sculpt fibers for moving long hair with a smooth sweeping.

This brush takes advantage of the

- New **Brush > Modifiers > Strength Multiplier** which helps to multiply the brush strength by whatever is configured in the slider, most especially long fibers to beautify hair. The length of the fiber can be preserved when this brush is used.

Groomer Strong

Though it has a considerably stronger effect on the fibers, this brush is somewhat comparable to the Groomer brush. a regular grooming brush that doesn't propagate in either direction. With just the root left to be protected, this brush can assist in persuading the majority of the fiber to be adopted.

Groom Clumps

This brush helps with clumping the tips of the fibers together or gives room for the tips to flare out based on the brush modifiers.

Groom Fast Lengthen

Reorients and modifies your fibers to follow the trajectory of your stroke. Because of the unique construction of this brush, you may change the length of your fibers without increasing the number of segments. Just like Groom Lengthen, but with less accurate distortion. Use this to find forms in a "quick and dirty" manner.

Groom Root Colorize

This brush Polypaintthe roots of the chosen fibers alone.

Groomer Magnet

Helps with deforming the tip of fibers to assimilate them together.

Groomer Twist

This rotates the fibers around the brush in a similar fashion such as twisting a lock of hair.

Groom Twist Slow

Other than its significantly slower operation, this brush is comparable to the Groomer Twist brush. It is important to note that low-speed strokes work best for this.

Groom Spike

This squeezes most of the affected fibers' lengths together in the creation of spikes.

Groom Spin Knot

This is the same as Groom Spike, except by lowering the Twist rate in the Brush palette, it has a softer, more progressive appearance. There is considerable effect when the fibers are brushed.

Pen brushes

There are various types of Pen brushes and they are all designed for working with QuickSketch and Polypainting.

- **PenA**: this is a soft stroke and subtle pen that widens with the application of pressure.

- **PenB**: this is very similar to PenA above but has a quite sharper inner line.

- **PenDots**: This is an intricate feathery stroke that, when drawn slowly, shows dots resembling lizard skin.

- **PenFur**: This is a delicate, intricate stroke that gets considerably wider after being drawn in a watercolor-like manner.

- **PenShadowSilver**: this is a brush that is quite sharper and crisper than Pen Shadow.

- **PenShadowSoft**: this is a brush that is darker and heavier than Pen Shadow.

- **PenShadow**: The Pen Shadow brush produces a line that resembles an engraving or pen and ink that is darkened on one side and lit on the other. responds favorably to pen pressure.

- **PenSketch:** this brush offers a soft and responsive stroke that widens upon the application of pressure. Similar to a brush with ink and wash.

- **PenSoft:** This is a much gentler Pen Sketch variant that spreads out considerably after drawing and releases a faint trail as though the paper has been moistened.

- **PenWetDots**: this is a wet paper version of Pen Dots, the stroke widens and also softens much after drawing.

- **PenWetSolid**: The PenWet Solid brush is characterized by its broad, straightforward stroke with a rounded edge that applies solid color with all but the lightest pressure.

- **PenWet**: With more pressure, the PenWet brush produces a wider and darker stippled stroke. Just like using a sloppy brush on damp paper.

Insert Mesh Brush

The DynaMesh procedure has made the Insert brush a powerful tool in your ZBrush toolkit. Several additional improvements have been added, including the capability to replace individual model components.

- It is possible to introduce a mesh as a negative while adding a model by stretching it in a direction perpendicular to the insertion while holding **ALT**. The mesh is integrated into the surface rather than being drawn on top of it.

Furthermore, the transformation of the original object will be retained in the duplicates if you apply the ALT modifier to one and then insert it in another.

- Simply insert the mesh and hit **the CTRL key** to restore it to its original size.

- Tap the **CTRL key** while adding the model to respect the basic inserted mesh proportions (1;1 ratio).

- When adding the model, press and hold the shift key to confine the insert mesh orientation to the model's closest world plane according to your viewing orientation.

The InsertMesh Object's orientation is saved when it is drawn (you can see this by switching to a transpose line after drawing an InsertMesh object out.)

- When holding **SHIFT**, creating a new **InsertMesh Object** will cause it to adopt the same orientation as the one you just created. It is necessary to design a new Transpose Line to return the orientation to a global axis. If you hold **SHIFT** and create another InsertMesh object, it will retain its previous orientation.

- The Z Intensity slider can be used to change the height of the inserted mesh. The mesh will remain vertical if the Z Intensity is kept constant at 100. When the Z Intensity value is less than 100, ZBrush will reduce the added mesh's height to accommodate the mesh.

- There's a new Projection Strength slider in the **Brush > Modifiers palette section.** The implanted mesh will naturally conform to the base surface when the value is high. If the value is kept low, the shape will remain unchanged.

Curve Bridge Brush

The Curve Bridge Brush automatically joins the edge points of the bridge to the base curves after creating a polygonal "bridge" between two previously created curves.

For the polygons in the bridge, a new PolyGroup is made. The support mesh has an automatically assigned mask that enables direct manipulation without affecting the mesh itself. This is similar to how the support mesh is automatically hidden by a mesh insert.

With this version, the Curve Bridge can recognize gaps, PolyGroups, and/or folded edges in the support mesh (Curve Frame capability). Once you've drawn two different curves, ZBrush will automatically create a polygon bridge linking the two surfaces.

Creating a bridge

The steps below can help with the creation of a bridge;

- Load the **LightBox > Tool > DemoHead**.

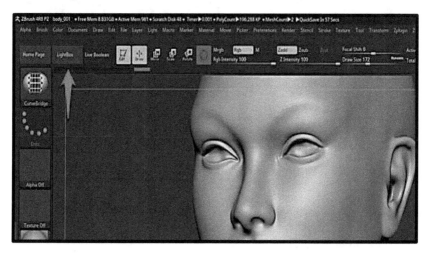

- When you get to **Tools > Geometry**, click on **Delete Lower** to take off all subdivision levels.

- Disable **Perspective (Hotkey P)** then snap the view to the side of the head by touching and holding the **Shift key** while also rotating the model.

- Select the **Slice Circle Curve brush**.

- Click the **CTRL + Shift** to call the **Slice Circle Curve to brush** then draw an ellipse close to the location of the ear. Now you should have a PolyGroup at the location of the ear.

- Tap **CTRL + Shift** and touch just once on the original PolyGroup. The ears of PolyGroup should be taken off.

- In **Tool > Geometry > Modify Topology**, Tap Delete Hidden to take off the ears entirely.

- Switch symmetry off by tapping **the X key**. Since the holes are already symmetrical, it is very unnecessary, and disabling them will also avoid unexpected results.

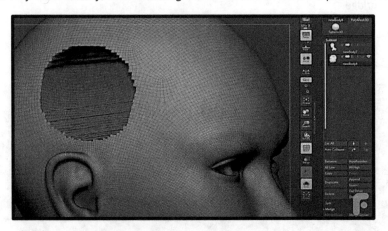

- Choose the **CurveBridge brush**.

- Make your opening stroke near the hole. Once your stroke reaches the first ear canal, depress the Shift key and let go. ZBrush will detect the gap automatically and draw an arc to hide it.

- Make use of the same method to create a curve around the second hole by rotating your model till you can see it.

- The bridge between the two holes will be created by ZBrush as soon as the cursor is released.

- Touch **once** on the surface to take off the curves.

- Remove **the mask if need be**.

Bridge Constraints

To properly implement the Bridge function, it is necessary to account for the model's current topology at the points where the bridge connects to the support **mesh. So, if you don't adhere to a few basic criteria, you may end up with topology irregularities:**

You have to always bridge the bends, whether they are closed or open. If you attempt to join a closed curve with an open curve using the Bridge brush, the result will be a flat polygon circle in the area where the open curve was. The result will be a non-manifold surface made up of overlapping polygons at the end.

Constraints on curve detection can be provided via PolyGroups, Crevasses, and Boundary openings, among other detection techniques. Curve identification may require multiple phases, with the Shift key used each time, depending on your data's topology and/or structure.

- Instead, you might try switching the Framing settings in the **Stroke > Curve Functions palette's toggle**.

Since this is the quickest and most effective method, the bridge is typically constructed in a straight line between the two arcs. The resulting polygons will be flat if the two curves you're combining are in the same plane. On an open surface, the tube's far and near polygons will overlap; on a closed surface, however, this will not occur.

ZSketch brushes

ZBrush offers many brushes that will generate a varied effect for your ZSketch. Several of them are fundamentally the same but have different settings such as Sketch 1, 2, and 3 which provide the same result with varied imbed depths.

Armature

You can draw ZSphere strips in any location in three dimensions using this brush. Using floating strips in this way is the best way to create huge body components such as arms and legs. This brush will draw on the working plane of the screen when you create a stroke; it will not line up with any existing ZSpheres.

Sketch 1, 2 and 3

These three brushes allow you to create Z-Sphere strips that, like the Armature brush, snap to the Z-Spheres below them.

With Sketch1 creating a line that is almost inside the underlying surface and Sketch3 producing a line that is almost outside of the surface, each of these three brushes yields a line with a distinct embedded depth.

Smooth 1, 2, 3 and 4

The smooth brushes work on the ZSketch ZSpheres by smoothing the ZSphere strip, with different behaviors at the start and finish of the strip, just like the standard smooth brush does in traditional sculpting. Smooth 1 allows you to enlarge and shift the end of the strip on the ZSphere or strip of ZSpheres underneath it.

Similar to how a conventional smooth brush behaves in traditional sculpting, the smooth brushes on ZSketch ZSpheres function by smoothing the ZSphere strip, with distinct behaviors at the start and finish of the strip. You can move and increase the end of the strip on the ZSphere or strip of ZSpheres underneath it using Smooth 1.

The Smooth 1, 2, 3 and 4 Brushes

Each ZSketch Smoothing outcome can be customized using the three sliders found in the Brush Palette> Smooth Brush Modifiers.

The setting Coverage Position determines how much a sketch's stroke is embedded into the underlying ZSpheres when smoothing is applied. This parameter will completely engulf the sketch in the underlying mesh or painting if you set it to 100.

The end strip's radius can be precisely met with the crossing mesh or drawing's radius by using the Converge Radius tool. The radius will be reduced to half the size of the related mesh or sketch if you enter a value of 50 here. Converge Color is a feature that changes the color of the end strip to match the connected sketch when it is turned on.

The Smooth brush that is now selected will be the one used whenever Shift is pressed unless a different Smooth brush is chosen.

To merge the stroke with the preceding ones when smoothing a ZSphere strip, keep the Shift key depressed when releasing the pen/mouse point.

Flush

The Flush brush aligns the strip of ZSpheres perfectly with the working plane of the screen by adjusting their radius and location. Using the **ALT key** in conjunction with the brush causes it to penetrate the model.

FlushDynamic

Except for the ZSphere strip being flattened and oriented to the pen tablet stroke rather than the screen working plane, the FlushDynamic brush produces the same effect as the Flush brush.

FlushResize

The FlushResize brush functions similarly to the Flush brush, except it ensures that all ZSphere strips are resized to the same size.

For best results, try using the Bulge and Flush brush after a Flush stroke has been applied.

Bulge

The bulge brushes will alter the radius of a strip, offering an inflated effect on the strip of ZSperes. Combined with the **ALT key**, the brush will offer a shrinking effect on your strip.

Bulge & Flush

Combining the Bulge and Flush tools, the Bulge & Flush brush flattens and resizes the ZSphere strip at the same time.

Use the Bulge & Flush brush after applying a flush stroke for optimal effects.

PushPull

The PushPull brush pushes the ZSphere strips outside of the underneath ZSpheres. When you hold the ALT key, it will move the ZSpheres into the underlying sketch/Mesh.

Fuse

The Fuse brush will bring together the clicked ZSphere with the closest strip of ZSpheres that exists. It will also give room for you to have a better continuation of existing strokes.

Alpha 3D Vector Displacement Meshes

Alpha textures are grayscale pictures that can be used with brushes to change how the surface geometry of the object is shifted. The launch of Alpha 3D is a logical advancement in this technology. ZBrush can use a 3D shape in this format to apply a stroke on a model and deform it. This method works best when an established shape needs to be copied, like when a dragon's horns need to grow from its skull.

It's very straightforward to produce microscopic characteristics with standard 2D alphas, such as skin pores, tiny scars, or fabric patterns. Basic shapes can be made with these 2D alphas, but they aren't tall enough to contain undercuts or overhangs.

The 3D Alpha feature is exempt from these limitations since it uses an existing mesh to deform the model's underside. The Alpha 3D system uses an internal 3D modeling technology called Vector Displacement Mesh (VDM).

The only restriction is the number of polygons needed to faithfully capture the brush's VDM shape. If you choose a low-quality mesh, there's a chance your model won't fit precisely within the brush's stored shape.

The above-discussed brushes are simply the categories of brushes that are in ZBrush. Heaven discussed that; let's have a look at the various types of brushes available in ZBrush;

Standard

The original ZBrush sculpting brush is the standard. This special brush helps with the displacement of outward vertices over which it passes when its modifiers are set to their default settings, giving the impression that clay has been added to a sculpture. Additionally, it works with every variety of brush modifiers available, including edit curves, strokes, and alphas.

The standard key will be carved into rather than built up by the model when you press the **Alt key.**

Move

This is applied when altering facial characteristics to convey feelings and create an asymmetrical face that looks more genuine. The mannequin can have a somewhat crooked smile and one eye that is slightly higher than the other with just three brushstrokes. When using brush modifiers, Move easily dismisses those that don't make sense.

Inflat

While the inflated brush stretches geometry by pushing vertices along their own normal, the Standard brush pulls or pushes geometry along the normal of the surface beneath the brush's center. This is helpful for sculptures where a lot of surface displacement is achieved with a small number of brushstrokes.

To create spikes, use the Std brush (left) and the Inflate brush (right) to inflate them. In both cases, all of the spikes were created simultaneously using the Spray stroke.

As opposed to the uniform orientation of standard spikes, which lie flat on the ground, inflating spikes stick straight up.

Elastic

This works just like the Inflate brush but due to some types of models, it is much more accurate at keeping the original shape of the surface like the surface is displaced. You can choose to experiment with the two to see which one works better for you.

Displace

Displace works just like the inflate brush but it works to maintain the details intact such that it will also suggest that the form underneath has swelled or has been displaced.

Magnify

The Magnify brush is similar to the Pinch brush in that it allows you to move vertices farther from the cursor while also giving you the option to move them up or down. The term "Magnify" refers to the way the vertices are displayed when the brush is being dragged using the DragDot stroke; they essentially give the impression of being magnified.

It is possible to independently modify the effects of displacement (pushing up) and magnification (pushing out). To Stretch out the vertices in a region of the plane without moving the surface, adjust Z Intensity to a high enough value and Magnify to 0.

Blob

The Blob brush works well for quickly producing some organic effects. In contrast to other brushes, its stroke uniformity is typically impacted by abnormalities in the surface beneath the stroke; in other words, it essentially creates short, irregular blobs, which gives rise to its name. If you use this on a smooth surface, it won't look like this. Whether the brush pushes the surface out or draws it in is determined by the blob slider.

Pinch

Vertices are brought together by the Pinch brush, which is the opposite of the Magnify brush and can be thought of as harsh. It is particularly helpful for adding hard edges to any form and for sinking in detail to create wrinkles and clothes. To ensure that the painter truly dips in detail or hardens the edge, the elevation slider has been added to the Pinch brush, allowing the artist to pinch in and out along the model's surface.

It's important to remember that Pinch and LazyMouse are frequently employed to create many passes and smooth, accurate ridges.

Flatten

Using the Flatten brush, you may quickly and easily "push down" portions of your model into flat surfaces. Moreover, you can change the surface's height as you press down.

You can give your model a rough flattening with the Flatten brush, like bringing the cheekbone plane to the forefront. You can also have flat surfaces for walls, mechanical models, etc.

For optimal results, make sure your brush is set to cover the entire area you wish to flatten and that your alpha is white.

When the flatten command is used, the angle at which the surface is flattened is determined by looking precisely beneath the center of the brush. Therefore, if you use this brush with strokes or alphas that change the angles of some areas of the surface, the flattening plane might move. If you wish to flatten to a certain plane, brush over a reasonably smooth region (maybe starting with the Smooth brush).

Clay

Clay Brush's primary function is to facilitate the sculpting of surfaces that employ alphas. Although other brushes can also be used for this, their primary function may cause some unintended consequences. Conversely, the clay brush will not yield some side effects because it is designed exclusively for sculpting with alphas.

When sculpting with a clay brush, the Z intensity and Clay slider settings have an impact on the final product.

Morph

The Morph brush is said to be active only when the model in use has a morph target that has been set. With this, the morph brush will brush the surface on which it is applied back toward the saved morph target surface.

Layer

The Layer brush will either raise (or decrease, if ZSub is on) the surface you are working on by the amount determined by the Z Intensity setting. One characteristic that distinguishes the layer brush is that when a stroke overlaps itself, the overlapped portions of the stroke do not go further displaced. The layer brush is your best option if you want to change the displacement of an entire layer without having to worry about unintentionally wiping your earlier work.

Nudge

To the degree that your model's density permits, you can move vertices around while they are still on the current surface by using the Nudge brush. By contrast, the Move brush does not alter the underlying surface; instead, it only moves vertices in the screen's XY plane. As an illustration: Envision creates a hole in the center of a tree. You can use the Magnify brush to quickly move vertices away from the knothole's center, do a local subdivision to add more geometry there, and then use Nudge to fine-tune the geometry so that it fits the knothole's slightly irregular shape to make the trunk's existing geometry flow around the new knothole.

Snake hook

You may easily remove protrusions from a 3D model, such as horns, tendrils, branches, and more, by using the SnakeHook brush. In the past, this task would have required more resources and taken a lot longer. DynaMesh, which can correct the stretched polygons brought on by the Snake Hook brush, works well with this brush.

Self-Evaluation Test

1. Highlight 5 of the various sculpting brushes in ZBrush and also mention some of the instances when these brushes can be used.

CHAPTER 3

INTRODUCTION TO DIGITAL SCULPTING

Introduction

Digital sculpting also referred to as sculpt modeling or 3D sculpting is widely known as the use of software that provides tools that can be used to push, pull, smooth, pinch, grab, or otherwise manipulate a digital object as though it were made of a real-life substance like clay.

Digital Sculpting

To depict the model, digital sculpting software can use a variety of geometric types, each with pros and cons. Most digital sculpting tools that are sold commercially use mesh-based geometry, where an object is represented by a movable surface mesh made up of interconnected polygons. This is similar in some respects to the real process of pounding copper plates to create a relief scene. Certain digital sculpting instruments employ voxel-based geometry, in which an object's volume is its primary constituent. It is possible to add and remove the material, just like in clay sculpting. Additional tools use many representations of the basic geometry.

Mesh-based applications have the important advantage of supporting several resolutions of sculpting on a single model. Larger polygons can be found in some highly detailed areas of the model, whereas smaller polygons can be found in other areas. The mesh can be changed at several degrees of detail in the majority of mesh-based systems, and changes made at one level will affect levels of model specificity that are both significantly higher and lower. When employing mesh-based sculpting, the amount of detail that may be added or altered might be limited by the mesh's established topology and the arrangement of its polygons.

One advantage of voxel-based systems is their ability to provide total form flexibility. As materials are added and removed throughout the sculpting process, the topology of the model can be changed, freeing the sculptor from having to take the object's surface layout polygons into account. After sculpting, the model might need to be retopologized to obtain a clean mesh for use in animation or real-time rendering. Nevertheless, voxels are more limited in their capacity to support various resolutions. Unlike mesh-based modeling, large changes made to voxels at a low degree of detail might destroy finer details.

Sculpting can most times introduce details specificity to meshes that would on the other hand have proved very difficult or impossible in the creation of the use of traditional 3D modeling techniques. This makes it preferable for the achievement of photorealistic and hyperrealistic results, though; many stylized results are achieved as well.

It may result in the production of the source meshes for video game models with low polygon count. When used with further 3D modeling and texturing methods, displacement mapping, and normal mapping, it can improve the appearance of gaming meshes frequently to the point of photorealism. Certain sculpting programs, such as Zbrush, Mudbox, and 3D-Coat, can be used with traditional 3D modeling and rendering programs. However, sculpting features are already present in 3D modeling applications such as 3ds Max, Maya, and MODO, albeit these are frequently less advanced than those found in applications dedicated to sculpting.

Digital sculpting is a tool used by both digital artists and sculptors to create models that are then printed using CNC technologies, such as 3D printing. The finished sculptures are frequently referred to as 3D printed art or digital sculpture. Although digital technology has advanced in many artistic fields (such as painting and photography), this is not as true for digital sculpture because of the sculpture's increased complexity and technological limitations.

Use of Symmetry in Digital Sculpting

By using symmetry, you can modify a side of your model while simultaneously updating the other side.

Three different types of symmetry exist, they are;

- Symmetry across an axis

- Poseable symmetry

- Radial symmetry

Note that the controls for symmetry can be found in the Transform palette.

Symmetry across an Axis

Symmetry across an axis can be referred to as the orientation of your model. **If you would like to have this feature turned on, follow the steps below;**

- Touch **Transform > Activate Symmetry**

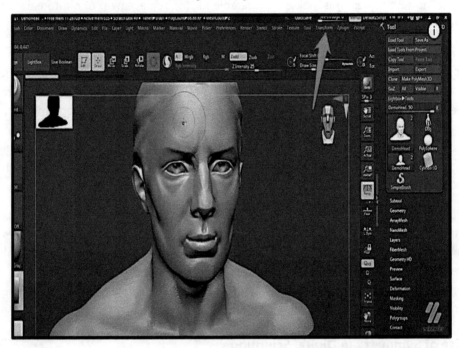

- Press either **X, Y, or Z** based on the axis you would like to have your actions mirrored across.

Poseable Symmetry

Poseable Symmetry may automatically generate symmetry based on topology instead of world space by utilizing ZBrush's SmartResym technology. Normal symmetry only holds if the model is the same shape along one of the X, Y, or Z axes. However, once situated, a model is not uniform along any axis and can't be symmetrically sculpted using traditional symmetry methods. Poseable Symmetry uses symmetry depending on your topology to address this. There must be axis symmetry in the topology. Consequently, it is unable to possess the two or more axis symmetry of a cube or sphere. This approach is dependent on the complete topological symmetry of your model and does not make use of UVs. All you need to do to use Poseable Symmetry is select which Transform Palette axis you want the symmetry to work across.

- Once done, press **Use Poseable Symmetry**.

For a more detailed process, follow the steps below;

- Press **Transform > Activate Symmetry**.

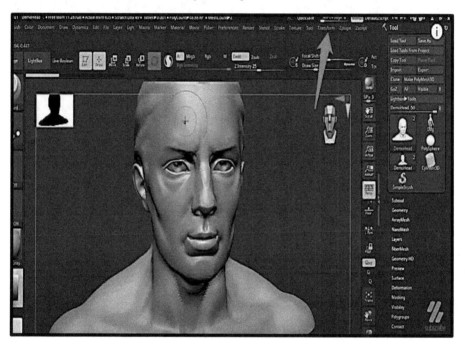

- Set **Tool > Geometry >SDiv** to the highest level of resolution you will be sculpting at.

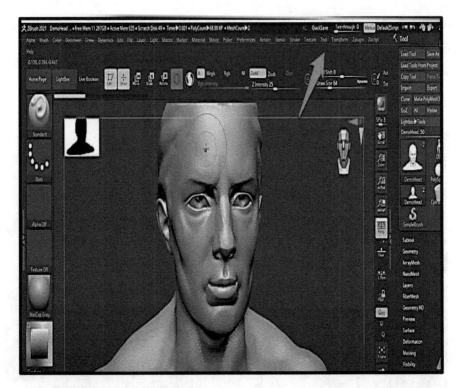

- Tap between **X, Y, and Z** based on the axis of the topology you would like to have your actions mirrored across.

- Press **Transform > Use Poseable Symmetry**.

Note

When a mesh that has Poseable Symmetry applied is divided, the symmetry property is lost and the mesh reverts to its original form.

To go back to Poseable Symmetry,

- Simply click **Use Poseable Symmetry** once more.

Likely, your model's edge looping is not the same on both sides if you are only getting roughly 50% symmetry and your model contains n-gons. Your model's edge looping may not be constant along its axis if it was created using earlier iterations of ZBrush and contained n-gons in the source mesh.

Radial Symmetry

Radial symmetry can be activated when the steps below are followed;

- Press **Transform > Activate Symmetry**.

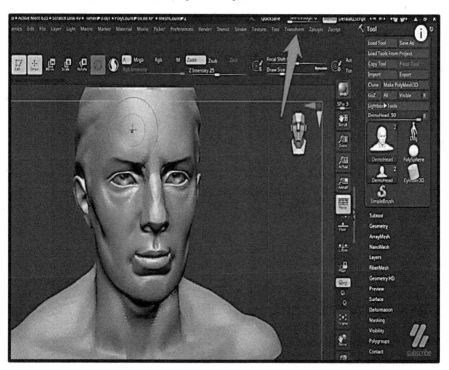

- Press between **X, Y, and Z** based on the axis you would like your actions mirrored across.

- Press **Transform > R**

- Configure Transform: Radial count to the number of times you would like to have your actions mirrored symmetrically along the surface.

Use of Alpha in Digital Sculpting

An alpha is a grayscale map of intensity. This can be used to express similar notions, the degree of masking, and the intensity level. Alphas are used to represent depth and height as bump and displacement maps in a variety of 3D modeling programs, such as ZBrush.

Note: Since ZBrush alphas are 16 bits deep, they may create far smoother grayscale gradations overall and in any area in which they are applied. Only 8-bit alphas are supported by some other programs, which can result in observable stair-stepping effects. Alphas in ZBrush is used for more than merely moving maps or bumps around. They can also have an impact on the shape of sculptures, masking, brush look, and the application of materials or colors.

You may also create your alphas and transform them into other tools like stencils (which are masking tools that offer diverse, and powerful, sets of capabilities).

In the section below, the most common method of getting and making use of alphas is highlighted.

Using Alphas

The geometry of common drawing tools is frequently determined by alpha values. This changes the pixel depth of the canvas. Sculpting brushes in 3D modeling software can have alphas applied to them to change the contour of the models. You can carry ZBrush's displacement and bump maps with you wherever you go by saving them as alphas.

Obtaining Alphas

ZBrush provides a wide range of helpful alphas that may be selected from the pop-up palette that appears when you click the big Current Alpha thumbnail, or from the Alpha Palette.

Using the Load Alpha button in the Alpha palette, you can also opt to load your images to use as alphas. Grayscale photos will be created from colored ones.

You could find it more convenient to simply paint a pattern on the screen and use the GrabDoc control to convert it to an alpha. Once the scene has been constructed, its depth will be converted to alpha. You may be certain of receiving a real 16-bit alpha using ZBrush's support for 16-bit depths.

Keep in mind that although alphas appear as thumbnails in the alpha pop-up palette, their actual size is always maintained. One way to create a small alpha is to paint on a huge canvas with the appropriate aspect ratio first, and then reduce the size of the canvas before adding the alpha. On the other hand, a large alpha can be useful if you want to consistently apply a lot of information over wide areas.

Tool Palette

The ZBrushCore project's 3D Models can be found in the Tool palette. Tools, or ZTools, are what you need to use them. (ZBrush isn't limited to just 3D models; it also has a variety of tools.)

The various tools that can be used will be listed in this section;

Copy Tool

The button of the Copy Tool can be used in the copying of the chosen model to memory with the inclusion of all of its sub-tools. With the use of the Paste Tool button, you can paste the copied model into the Tool palette. A tool can be copied between projects.

Paste Tool

The button of the Paste Tool is used basically in the pasting of any of the models that have been copied.

Import

The import button helps with the importing of a 3D mesh from an OBJ file.

Export

You can export models in OBJ and other 3D formats by using the Export Tool button.

Clone

This button aids in creating a precise replica of the selected model. Only the selected sub-tool will be replicated if the model has sub-tools.

Make PolyMesh3D

- With a click of the **Create Polymesh3D button,**

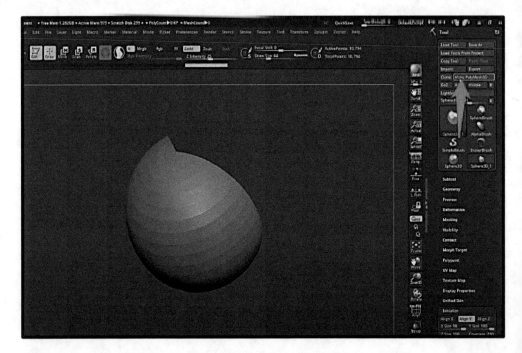

A new poly mesh object will be generated that is geometrically similar (in terms of size and polygon resolution) to the selected 3D primitive. This item has been included in the Tool palette.

All mathematical information utilized to define the shapes of primitive objects will be reset if the Initialize sliders are adjusted. When it comes to texturing and manipulating, polygonal meshes are very versatile. They can be built with a variety of mesh resolutions, which makes it easier to create displacement and normal maps.

The mesh resolution of ZSphere-generated Polymesh3Ds is identical to that of the equivalent Adaptive Skins.

The Tool palette has various sub-palettes and some are discussed in the section below;

Sub-tool

SubTools are individual polygonal objects. Each SubTool allows you to use the maximum amount of polygons your computer is capable of processing. If your computer is capable of handling 8 million polygons, you can use 4 SubTools to create a model with up to 32 million polygons. Subtools, on the other hand, are autonomous. You cannot pose or sculpt many SubTools at once.

Subtools are always shown in a list. There are about eight SunTools displayed; modify the scrollbar to the left if you would like to display more SubTools.

You can hide Subtools by turning off the eye icon close to their name in the list. You can also use the Solo mode to hide all sub-tools except the one in use.

Geometry

- **Lower Res:** Among the available mesh resolutions for this object, choosing the **Lower Subdivision Resolution** option will select the mesh with the next-lowest resolution. Choose the **Divide button in the Geometry palette** to add a higher-resolution mesh. Using the Density slider in the Adaptive Skin panel, you can choose the highest possible mesh resolution if this tool is a ZSphere object in Preview mode.

- **Higher Res**: You can select the highest-resolution mesh that is available for this object by clicking the Higher Subdivision Resolution option. Select the Divide button from the Geometry palette to include a mesh with more resolution. If this tool is a ZSphere object in Preview mode, you can select the maximum mesh resolution using the Density slider in the Adaptive Skin panel.

- **SDiv slider**: The Subdivision Level slider can be used to select an alternate mesh resolution. The coarsest mesh available will be utilized when set to 1. Select the Divide button from the Geometry palette to include a mesh with more resolution. If this tool is a ZSphere object in Preview mode, you can select the maximum mesh resolution using the Density slider in the Adaptive Skin panel.

- **Del Lower**: To get rid of any lower-resolution meshes that might be associated with this item, click the **Remove Lower Subdivision Level button**. Choose the Divide button in the Geometry palette to add a higher-resolution mesh.

- **Del Higher**: If you click the Remove Higher Subdivision Level option, any higher-resolution meshes that were previously available for this object will be deleted. Choose the **Divide button** in the Geometry palette to add a higher-resolution mesh.

48

Masking

Options for masking a 3D object can be found under the

- **Tool > Masking section of the main palette**.

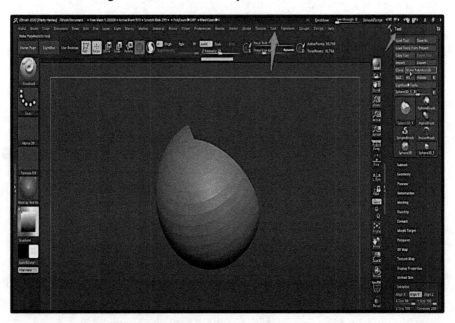

All sculpting and painting operations, whether performed directly or changed in the Deformation palette, are affected by masking.

It's possible to use a mask in two different ways:

- By holding the **CTRL key**, paint the mask right onto the object. By holding down **Ctrl**, a variety of masking brushes can be selected.

- Drag while holding **CTRL** to project the selected Alpha onto the item. You can pick whichever letter of the alphabet you like by holding down the Control key.

When the View Mask toggle is activated, the masking for the current SubTool is displayed.

You can use masking to stop some parts of a 3D object from being changed. An object's mask manifests as a darker region on its surface; the mask's strength is determined by the extent of this darkness.

- If you're in Edit mode (and have Drawn Pointer selected), you can also paint a mask onto an item by pressing and holding **the Ctrl key** while you paint.

- Another useful feature is the ability to use the current Alpha as a mask by clicking and dragging from outside the item while holding **the Ctrl key**.

Projection Master

Projection Master is a unique feature of ZBrush that gives room for you to make use of the 2D and 2.5D brushes in sculpting, texturing and otherwise having to work with your 3D model.

The Projection Master's concept is very simple and easy to understand. You use Projection Master when working with a 3D model to turn the visible portion of your model into pixels on the canvas. This will instantly sample the depth of your model at each position on the screen that is visible, and it will change every matching pixel to display the material, color, and depth of the model at that precise location. When finished, the model will be removed from the canvas so you can work with the model's pixel-based representation. This process is known as **dropping the model to the screen**. Upon the completion of your sculpting, painting, etc. you can then employ the use of Projection Master in the picking up of the model. This will map the modified pixels back to the original mode and will also transfer the changes in both color and depth.

Numerous new possibilities arise from the ability to modify the model's final geometry using any paintbrush. For example, you can use the Blur brush to soften a region of your model that is too rough by turning off the RGB channel.

Generally speaking, to use Projection Master, you drop the model, focus on the side that is facing you, pick it up, rotate it slightly, drop it again, and so on. As a result, you may quickly transfer as much data as you can from the model to the canvas pixels.

Please be aware that Projection Master is a vast improvement over the 3D Copy feature and can be used in place of it for virtually all purposes.

Using Projection Master

Pressing the g key or the Projection Master Button, which is located in the top left corner of the ZBrush window in the default configuration, will launch Projection Master.

You will exit Projection Master once you have finished painting and have done the same thing twice.

A texture map needs to be applied to every model that you wish to utilize with Projection Master. If you haven't set a texture map to your model yet, you will be given the option to do so automatically.

The Projection Master Dialogue box opens when a model is dropped and then opens again when it is picked up. You can choose which properties to transfer, how to transfer them, and what to send (for instance, you can decide to have your work on the canvas change the geometry of the model but not its color).

The two spheres in the Projection Master dialog provide visual input on how the selected parameters will impact the transfer of details to and from your model.

With Projection Master, you also have online help that shows all of the details embedded in this option; simply press the button located at the lower right corner of the Projection Master dialog.

Pixol to Polygon Ratio

Before "dropping" your model into Projection Master, it's best to resize it such that the area of a visible polygon is roughly equal to the area of a pixel on the canvas. Since Projection Master does not generate new polygons, any geometry contained inside an area greater than a single pixel will be "transferred" back to a single polygon that retains its flatness. This can cause some of your finer details to be lost in the re-creation process.

Furthermore, if your model is one in which lots of polygons cover just one pixol, the situation will be the inverse of the above-described situation; this is so because you can only paint a single pixol, and any details created on that pixol will be transferred to all of the polygons underneath it, more or less in a uniform manner. Hence when you leave from your model to the Projection Model and back, there is a tendency for you to lose details on your model.

Controls

Most of the options in the Projection Master dialog box relate to scenarios when you are painting or detailing at a model's edge, or on a portion of the model where the plane's normal at that point points far away from you instead of toward you. Ideally, you should rotate your model so that the area of interest faces you, then drop it to paint and detail that area, pick it back up and rotate it to the next area of interest, drop it, and so on, to get the most out of Projection Master. You can safely ignore the majority of the following setup settings if you proceed in this manner.

Colors Option

This doesn't need so much explanation. When this option is turned on, any color painted on the canvas while having Projection Master active will be sent back to the texture map of the model anytime the model is picked up.

Material Option

This and the Color choice are rather similar. Models in ZBrush can have both a material map and a texture map in addition to the one default material. Any paint you apply on the canvas when you drop a model with the Materials toggle enabled will be copied to the object's materials map.

Certain materials take into account a model's texture, whereas others do not. Therefore, when applying color and material to a model, the material may completely cover up any texture or may allow some texture to show through.

It's also important to note that rotating the model modifies the way materials appear. This is caused, aside from reflected material, by the fact that ZBrush materials are calculated at each point based on that point's location; as a result, when anything rotates or moves, its point locations change, and each point's appearance of the material will also change.

Fade Option

The Fade option affects just how color is added when texturing a model or how deformations are smoothed in parts of a model.

Effects of Fade on Texturing

When a texture or color is painted onto a handicapped model, it is distributed evenly throughout the model upon picking it up. Since painted regions will have the same hue throughout, this is especially true for pure colors.

The surface color will fade based on the angle the model creates with the standard screen if the Fade feature is enabled. This method of using the airbrush is similar to painting by misting paint onto a screen. Ordinarily, the model's surfaces perpendicular to the screen will get less paint than those parallel to it.

Deformation Option

If this is enabled, any modifications made to the pixol depths in Projection Master will be carried over and will impact the model's polygon placements the next time the model is lifted. The only noteworthy thing about this option is that it assumes a flawless mastery of the Pixol to Polygon Ratio.

With this setting in the Projection Master, ZBrush can sculpt incredibly detailed models with a high polycount. You will almost always see this option switched on if this is the type of detailing you are doing.

Normalize Option

The Normalize option is most noticeable when you are using Projection Master to make significant changes to your model, like sculpting high heights or deep indentations, or when you are sculpting in the direction of the object's boundaries. Normalize has made displacements made in Projection Master apply perpendicularly to the model's surface at the point of application, instead of drawing in or out from the canvas's center.

When working on a surface that needs precise detailing and is roughly facing you, leave Normalize switched off. Just consider this: the reasoning is simple. For example, if you are adding more detail to a section of skin that already has scars sculpted into it, the scar margins may face different directions, even though the piece of skin as a whole may be facing you.

Using Projection Master to add further features on top of the scars with normalizing on may cause parts of that detailing to be pushed "sideways" into regions of the scars, depending on the direction of the scar surface. If the scar surface suddenly shifts orientation over a brief distance, visual abnormalities could result. Under extreme circumstances, even surface interpenetration is feasible.

Array Mesh

You can construct multiple instances of geometry in various patterns and shapes with ZBrush's Array Mesh system, which is essentially an array of systems. This tool allows you to modify the original mesh's structure in real time or change the array's modifiers. You may rapidly create sophisticated instanced geometry by utilizing the sliders in the Array Mesh sub-palette.

Arrays can be stacked on top of one another thanks to the multi-staged Array Mesh concept. The simplicity of use in building Instanced shapes with this technology is unmatched by tank treads or complete skyscrapers.

Due to the instanced nature of the Array Mesh, any modifications made to the original model will be reflected in the entire Array immediately. If you would like to add curtains to all the windows in an Array you made for a building's facade by making a single change to the model.

Array Mesh Stages

An Array Mesh can be built using several steps, or a single complicated action. The location and content of the previous stage can be utilized in further stages; the latter simply has to be sent along at the start of a new stage.

The steps of the Array Mesh are independent of one another. This makes it possible to change stage-specific traits.

Tank track treads are a good illustration because;

- The first stage is a definition of the top flat part.

- The second stage defines one of the rounded parts.

- The third stage is a definition of the lower flat part.

- The fourth stage defines the other rounded part and also helps with its connection to the beginning of the first stage copy.

- The fifth stage is a definition of a mirrored version of the entire track to bring up two full threads.

With editing the source mesh, the tracks can be updated in real-time automatically.

Array Mesh and Nano Mesh

Array mesh and Nano mesh are two different functions that can work together in two different ways; Duplicate a NanoMesh with an Array Mesh or make use of an Array Mesh as placement polygons for Nanos.

Duplicating a NanoMesh with an ArrayMesh

A NanoMesh is the same as utilizing real geometry while using ZBrush. This means that it can be used to create an Array Mesh without first turning the NanoMesh instances into geometry.

Any modifications made to the source object of the NanoMesh will be mirrored in the final NanoMesh and then repeated across the Array Mesh because of the common instanced geometry foundation between NanoMesh and Array Mesh.

Converting an Array Mesh to a NanoMesh

Using several copies of the same object, an Array Mesh is a great tool for creating parametric forms. The ultimate shape of an Array Mesh will be rather consistent because it makes copies of the original item. By converting each Array Mesh copy into a NanoMesh, you may leverage the different parameters in the NanoMesh system to achieve a more organic-looking design.

An ArrayMesh can be converted to a NanoMesh by taking each array instance and placing it into a single placement polygon. Once the Array Mesh is changed, all of the NanoMesh functionality is accessible, including changing the original model, applying randomizations, and swapping out other NanoMeshes.

A very simple workflow can be;

Make an ArrayMesh in one step or several steps. Create a NanoMesh version of the above. Once the conversion is complete, you can adjust the number of instances or apply additional ArrayMesh modifiers.

Choose an **Insert brush, Insert Multi Mesh brush (IMM), or NanoMesh brush**. Click on the **M key** to choose the 3D model of your choice.

Select **Tool > NanoMesh > Replace NanoMesh** from Bush. The 3D model associated with the placement polygons will then be replaced.

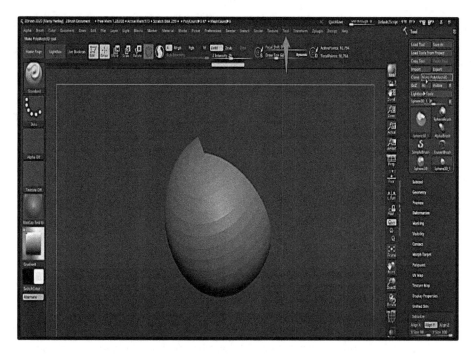

Make use of all the NanoMesh settings to refine the results interactively.

ArrayMesh Presets

The ArrayMesh's settings can be shared with other artists or stored as a file on your computer for later use. Another option is to save these files in the ZArray Mesh folder. LightBox's Array tab will make the ArrayMesh accessible after you place it in this folder.

It only takes two clicks on the thumbnail of an ArrayMesg preset from LightBox to apply it. Next, ZBrush will automatically select the Tool that you are now using, activate the ArrayMesh feature, and add the default ArrayMesh settings.

ArrayMesh Settings

Below are some of the ArrayMesh settings that you can modify for more control over the process of duplication. Note that most of these settings are interactive which enables you to freely experiment with advanced multiple-stage creations.

Transpose

If you flip the TransPose switch, you can use the TransPose system to perform interactive operations on your Array Mesh.

By selecting Move, Scale, or Rotate with TransPose active, you'll reveal the TransPose Action Line and be able to tweak the Array Mesh's Offset, Scale, and Rotate settings, respectively. (The Amount Sliders for X, Y, and Z.)

Additionally, when utilizing TransPose mode with an Array Mesh, the location of the transformation's center of mass can be interactively determined. To change the pivot point, drag and click the yellow circle at the start of the TransPose line.

Regarding the camera's operating plane, the pivot can be freely shifted in any direction. Use the orthographic view and carefully choose your vantage point if you want to position the pivot indication exactly where you want it. The Action Line will adjust to fit the new place when you move the pivot point.

Lock Position, Lock Size

An Array Mesh's "Lock Position" and "Lock Size" options prevent the position from being changed without starting over and creating a new array.

By default, changes are made to the main model, and the placements are subsequently scaled or resized to correspond. When this locking mechanism is engaged, the present positions cannot expand or move. These locks result in all linked stages with the array being locked.

Exchange X for Y, X for Z, and Z for Y

Depending on the viewpoint plane from which you are currently observing the model, the axis orientation can be switched between X, Y, and Z using the Switch X, Switch Y, and Switch XZ commands. These operations come in handy when you need to apply a transformation that might not be aligned with the global axis.

Transform Stage

The slider of the **Transform Stage** can enable you to navigate between the various stages of ArrayMesh. If you would like to create a new stage, make use of the **Append New or Insert New functions**.

When an ArrayMesh is initially created, this slider will be grayed out because there are no additional stages to pick from.

Append New

After every step that already exists in the list, this stage produces a new one. This indicates that this button will assist in creating a fifth level if you have four stages and are presently in the first.

Insert New

When you pick **Insert New,** a new stage is added after the stage you have selected. For example, if you have four stages and are currently on the first, clicking this button will generate a new stage 2 and the subsequent stages will each increase by one. This feature allows you to place a new stage in between two already existing ones.

Reset

This option sets all parameters for the stage you have currently chosen back to their default values.

Delete

When you press Delete, the active stage will be removed. If that's the only level, the Array Mesh will be removed and reset to its initial state.

Copy, Paste

While working with Array Meshes, you may use the Copy and Paste capabilities to quickly and easily transfer parameters from one stage to another.

Repeat

To choose the required number of duplicates to be produced from the present model, use the Repeat slider. Set the slider to 2 to create a single clone, as this value always includes the original model.

Chain

As soon as one phase concludes, the next one begins thanks to the chain effect. Using a single-instanced mesh spanning numerous phases, complex curve structures may be generated with ease.

The Alignment and Pattern settings are disabled when the Chain option is selected.

Offset

The Offset mode consists of the X, Y, and Z Amount sliders and curves together. The duplicates will move away from the original once the option is enabled by changing the sliders. How far the instance created at this stage is from the original object is indicated by the Offset value.

The curve can be changed to change the speed or slowness of the distances between duplicates throughout the array's length. Any adjustments you make to the curve will show up on the screen right away. Moving the TransPose line in Move mode is all that is required to interactively change the Offset values when in TransPose mode.

Scale

The Scale mode interacts with the X, Y, and Z Amount sliders and curves. Activating this feature allows you to scale the copies up or down concerning the original by simply adjusting the sliders. The Scale parameter indicates how much larger or smaller the original is compared to the output copy.

The curve's form determines how quickly or slowly the spacing between duplicates changes as one travels the length of the array. Any adjustments you make to the curve will show up on the screen right away.

You can dynamically modify the Scale settings by using the TransPose line if you switch to Scale mode while in TransPose mode.

Pivot

The X, Y, and Z curves as well as the Amount slider can be utilized in this mode. Adjusting the sliders (Offset, Scale, and Rotate) will move the transformation's pivot point if the checkbox is checked. The pivot point remains constant despite variations in the curvature.

When TransPose is enabled, changing the Pivot values only requires selecting the TransPose Move mode and dragging the origin's yellow circle.

See the TransPose and Pivot section of the previously referenced papers for more reading on the pivot.

Extrude

This mode helps with the conversion of the actual ArrayMesh results to a new mesh and generates between each former instance, depending upon its PolyGroups.

For this function to be performed, the ArrayMeshobjects ought to share PolyGrouping on their opposite sides. The MakeMesh function will observe the PolyGrouping and design bridges between the same PolyGrouped areas whenever Extrude is enabled. When creating environment elements like stairs or organic models like snakes, this method comes in handy because it fills in the gaps created between the repeats. Nearby instance duplicates will be combined into one by ZBrush. If this is not the intended result, click Create Mesh again after adjusting the array's Repeat Value to leave more space between instances.

Tutorial

ZBrush has an advanced array system called ArrayMesh that lets you duplicate geometry instances in different forms and patterns. As you modify the original meshes of the array's modifiers' structures, this functionality adapts in real-time. Using Transpose with ArrayMesh or the sliders in the ArrayMesh sub-palette, complex instanced geometry can be quickly constructed. There is also a multi-step mechanism in the ArrayMesh system for layering several arrays inside of each other. You can easily develop instanced shapes, like tank treads or entire buildings, with this framework!

Self-Evaluation Test

1. Make a digital sculpture with the use of symmetry.

2. Make a digital sculpture applying Alpha.

3. Mention the various options available for use in the Tools palette.

4. Highlight what the projection master is all about.

CHAPTER 4

SUBTOOLS AND FIBERMESH

Introduction to Subtools in ZBrush

SubTools are discrete polygonal objects. Each SubTool may have as many polygons as your hardware will allow it to handle. Your model can have 32 million polygons if your machine can handle 8 million polygons and you have four SubTools.

SubTools come particularly handy for assembling a model made up of discrete parts. For example, the clothing and body of a character model may be two different subtools. SubTools makes it simple to concentrate on a single component at a time, increasing efficiency and allowing you to save up hard drive space.

SubTool Subpalette

Visibility Sets

- When you click **the eye icon** of the chosen SubTool, it will turn off the visibility for the entire Subtool.

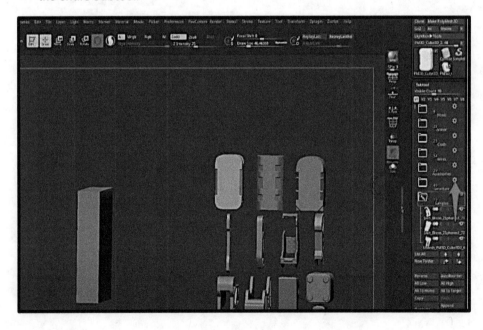

List All

This option helps to make a list of all SubTools in alphabetical order in a pop-up menu.

New Folder

With the use of this option, you can range the SubTools in another folder. Or have them arranged according to their function.

Arrow Buttons

Up arrow

Choose the **next SubTool** up in the SubTool list.

Down arrow

Choose the **next SubTool** down in the SubTool list.

Up and over the arrow

Moves the **chosen SubTool** down in the list.

Down and over the arrow

Move the **chosen SubTool** down in the list.

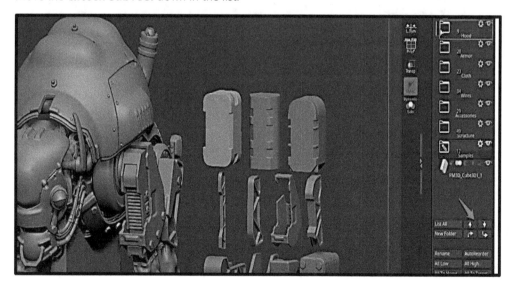

Rename

When you press **the rename feature**, it changes the name of the currently chosen **SubTool**.

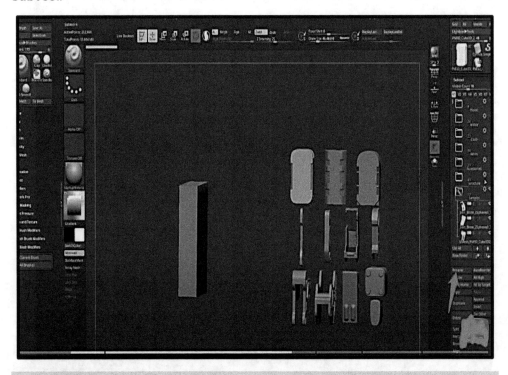

AutoReorder

The AutoReorder function alters the order of the SubTools in the list by ranking them according to their polygon counts. SubTools with bigger polygon counts will be put above SubTools with smaller polygon counts.

All Low

This button automatically configures all SubTools to their lowest subdivision level.

All High

This button automatically configures all SubTools to their highest subdivision level.

Duplicate

This button helps with the duplication of the chosen **SubTool** and includes it beneath the chosen SubTool.

Append

Anytime you touch the **append button**, a new **SubTool** will be added to the list. Select your favorite model from the pop-up menu, and it will be appended to the end of the list. ZBrush Primitives can be sculpted immediately after being instantaneously transformed into poly meshes.

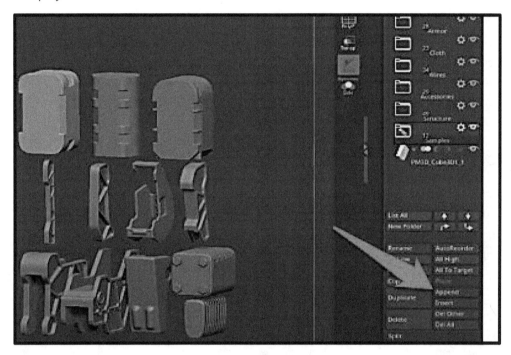

Insert

A new SubTool will be added to the list underneath the SubTool that is presently selected when you click **Insert**. Choose the model you want to integrate from the selection that shows up. ZBrush Primitives can be sculpted right away because they instantly become poly meshes.

Delete

When you want to get rid of the **selected SubTool,** press **Delete**. Using this option will delete the specified SubTool but will not affect any other SubTools. Be aware, though, that this operation cannot be undone or the SubTool restored; the SubTool will be permanently removed.

A Tool's complete removal from the Tool menu indicates that all of its SubTools have been eliminated; the Polymesh3D Star will take the place of the last SubTool. This is the strategy to utilize if you want to make your ZBrush project file smaller overall.

Del Other

Except for the selected SubTool, all SubTools will be removed when you click this button. It is important to note that the SubTools have been completely erased; neither the operation nor the SubTools may be undone.

Del All

You can remove the **Tool from the Tool palette** and all of its sub-items with a click on **the Del All** button (the final SubTool will be replaced by the Polymesh3D Star). This is also the strategy to utilize if you want to minimize the total size of your ZBrush project file. Kindly note that deleting SubTools is irreversible and cannot be undone or the SubTools recreated.

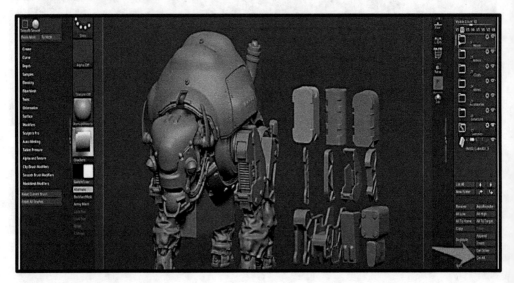

Split

Split Hidden

This button will help with the splitting of the chosen **SubTool** into two different SubTools such that the hidden part of the mesh and the visible part will become different SubTools.

Groups Split

Clicking the Groups Split button will split each polygroup linked to the chosen SubTool into a separate SubTool. If the Split is performed with the SubTool set to the maximum subdivision level, the subdivision levels will be maintained.

Split to Similar Parts

Depending on the number of vertices in each mesh component, pressing this button will divide the selected SubTool into new SubTools. This is primarily helpful for mesh separation following the application of the InsertMesh or Topology brushes.

Split to Parts

This option will divide all mesh shells into different SubTools.

Split Unmasked Points

The Split Unmasked Points option, when selected, will split the selected SubTool in half, resulting in two new SubTools: one with only the masked points and the other with only the unmasked points.

Split Masked Points

This option will split the chosen SubTool into two different SubTools such that the masked aspect of the mesh and the unmasked aspect of the mesh will be different SubTools.

Merge

MergeDown

This button will bring together the **chosen Subtool** with the SubTool directly beneath the list.

MergeSimilar

All of the SubTools with the same polygon count will be merged into a single one when you click the MergeSimilar button. Combining comparable SubTools in this way is beneficial. This cannot be reversed.

Merge Visible

When you **click MergeVisible**, all of the currently visible SubTools will be merged into a single Tool in the Tool palette, with a name composed of the prefixes Merged_ and the name of the first visible SubTool. There is a correlation between this action and the Weld setting.

Boolean

Boolean systems, for all their power, have traditionally required a tremendous lot of trial and error before producing an adequate result. With Live Boolean, artists may combine numerous sculptures and view the final mesh in real-time. All models are subtracted from each other, independent of the number of polygons in each.

You may also use Live Boolean with the instancing tools that ZBrush currently offers, such as ArrayMesh and NanoMesh. Even better, you may use Live Boolean to shape your models as you examine the Boolean results.

Any of these capabilities can be used to create new ZBrush-exclusive sculpting methods.

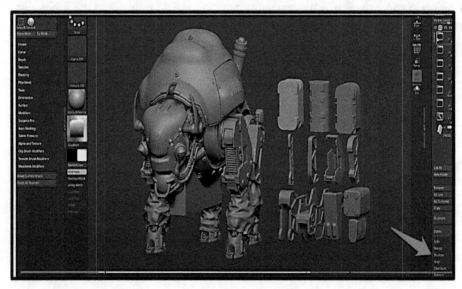

BevelPro

With the new BevelPro plugin, low-poly modeling is not necessary to create complex bevels for models of any resolution. For medium-to-high-quality meshes, BevelPro works well. It lets you choose which edges to bevel by using masking and Polygroups. Adjust and examine your results non-destructively, and even generate your bevels as separate segments of geometry for use with Live Boolean.

Remesh

Remesh All

When you click the **Remesh All button**, a new mesh will be generated by skinning the currently active SubTools. Each SubTool's Union, Difference, and Intersection parameters will be taken into account during this procedure. A new SubTool with the generated mesh will be appended to the existing ones.

During the skinning process, symmetry can be utilized by activating the X, Y, and Z axis indicators located in the button's upper portion.

Res

The Resolution slider helps to determine the polygon resolution of the new mesh when you press the Remesh All option. Higher resolution will need more time for computing.

Polish

While a Remesh All operation is in progress, the polish slider aids in controlling the amount of polish added to the new mesh. The circle icon that is situated on the right side of the slider can be used to choose between two distinct polish modes.

The open circle will give the SubTools a polished look while maintaining their overall form and volume.

Without maintaining the volume, a closed circle offers a finish that will smooth the skin.

PolyGrp

The Remesh All operation will build new polygroups depending on the intersection of the original SubTools if the PolyGrp switch is enabled. If you don't want polygroups in the new mesh, disable this switch.

Project

Project All

The projection of sculptural detail from a source mesh to a designated mesh is aided by this process. While broad shape similarity is required, similarity in topology is not a requirement for the meshes. The source and target meshes should be the only two Subtools accessible and should be in the same list as other Subtools. The projection's breakdown will be impacted by the additional settings contained in this section.

Dist

This setting affects the projection distance for each normal from the source mesh to the target mesh. 1 is said to be the maximum setting.

Mean

The mean slider will obtain the average of the point difference between the target mesh and the source mesh and configure it as the plateau for Project All.

ProjectionShell

The ProjectionShell slider will provide the target mesh start point for ProjectAll.

The source mesh in the picture is the gray dog, and the target mesh is the red dog. The red dog's ProjectionShell has been raised, allowing the Inner ProjectAll to be used to project data accurately.

ZBrush will only project to the source mesh from inside the Projection Shell when the Inner option is selected and the ProjectionShell setting is used. If any of the gray dogs stayed away from the red dogs, they would not be taken.

Extract

By "extracting" geometry from a particular region of a model, Mesh Extraction generates a new mesh. For a smooth, even boundary, the edge is cleaned, but the majority of the topology is repeated. Occasionally, during this operation, triangle polygons at the rounded corners may be employed. You can either mask or hide a section of the mesh to indicate the part to be extracted.

FiberMesh in ZBrush

The fiber mesh is a unique mesh generation tool. In contrast to the Fiber material, Fiber mesh is not a render process. Rather, Fiber mesh designs real geometry on the fly which you can add to the existing model as a new SubTool.

Depending on your criteria, the FiberMesh sub-palette lets you create a wide variety of shapes for fibers, hair, fur, and even plants. Since these fibers are a real geometry, you may then sculpt your hair using ZBrush's extensive feature set. This includes the ability to paint them using the usual sculpting brushes, Masks, TransPose, and the PolyPaint system. Additionally, a range of specialized "Groom" brushes are available specifically designed to be used with the FiberMesh feature.

These fibers can be exported to any application of your choice because they are real geometry. Exporting the fiber geometry will allow for the application of a texture to each fiber, whether or not UVs are used.

The geometry of FiberMesh is designed for performance and has particular characteristics that help with informing the ZBrush groom sculpting brushes that they are being used on a FiberMesh.

- With settings in the **Brush > FiberMesh sub-palette**, any 3D brush can be modified to modify fibers. ZBrush transforms the FiberMesh into a conventional poly mesh if you alter the topology, such as by slicing the fibers or adding subdivision levels. After that, the sculpting brushes will function just like they would for a typical mesh object.

Tutorial 1

Characters, mechanical items, and other tools can grow intricate, and it is frequently faster to build them from discrete components than as a single whole. Each piece is known as a sub-tool and is maintained via the toolbar.

A character's body, for instance, could be one sub-tool, his helmet, another, his sword, and so forth. You can only sculpt with one Subtool at a time, and it is the only one that is ever active. You can choose a different sub-tool by either clicking on it or by utilizing the Up and Down arrows located beneath the list. You can combine two subtools into one by moving the one you've selected up and down the list order using the curved arrows.

With the button, you can rename subtools; because most will begin with 'sphere' or 'cube,' this can be useful.

All Low and All High are used to simultaneously change each sub-tool's subdivision level. (Subdivision levels add to the sculpt's polycount; you can select between high levels for intricate detail work and low levels to alter the object's general contour.) A sub-tool that already exists can be duplicated using Duplicate and then moved.

Append adds a new sub-tool to the end of the list. Insert will put it under the tool that you are now using. Pressing the Delete key will delete the selected tool from the list.

In the Split Section, you can arrange tools into sub-tools according to their poly group configurations (see below). The opposite is achieved in the Merge section, which lets you combine two or more subtools. Because merge down will combine the selected tool with the tool right behind it, the sub-tool order is very important.

NB: Several icons are present next to every sub-tool. Toggle the visibility of selected canvases on the screen by using the eye symbol when working with small portions of detailed models. The Additive, Subtractive, and Intersection modes—which control how sub-tools interact with each other when they are merged—are represented by the first three icons.

NB: There is a Taskbar Plugin called 'Subtool Master' that will provide you with a few additional organizational choices when working with your sub-tools.

Self-Evaluation Test

1. Describe subtools in ZBrush stating what they can be used for.

2. Make use of some of the sub-tools palette in sculpting.

3. Make use of FiberMesh in ZBrush .

CHAPTER 5

ZSPHERES

Introduction

ZSpheres is a well-known sophisticated ZBrush tool that makes it easy and quick to sketch up a 3D model, particularly one that is organic.

After the model has been fully formed using ZSpheres, it can be skinned in preparation for additional sculpting. ZSpheres are unlike anything else in some other 3D software, and you can only become familiar with them by using them.

There are various sub-tools to e

ngage in if you would like to work with ZSpheres;

- Press the **Subtool > Append button** for the model you are dealing with and choose the ZSphere tool from the menu that pops up.

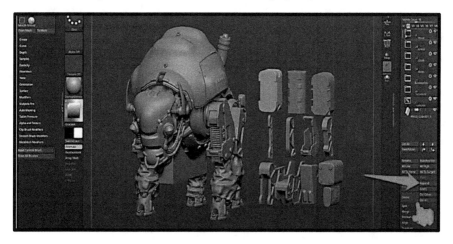

- Change to the new **ZSphere subtool.** Toggle on subtool transparency such that you will be able to see what you are doing.

- With the use of Scale and Move modes, you can resize and also reposition the ZSphere to suit.

Model with ZSpheres normally when the subtool Transparency is turned on. Select and move to add zspheres that match the other subtools' surfaces while the transparency of the subtool is turned off. Select a new start zsphere by selecting it in Move mode.

Display properties

Below are a few of the display properties in ZSphere;

Density

This slider helps to determine the number of gray link spheres that are drawn between parent ZSpehers while the edit is ongoing.

Color

The ZSphere object's link-sphere display is impacted by the Color Intensity slider. The slider controls the percentage intensity of the parent colors to be used. Typically, they are presented darker than the parent ZSpheres. Full-color intensity is displayed if this slider is set to 100%.

Size

When modifying a ZSphere model that is tightly packed, the Display Size slider comes in pretty handy. It aids in determining the relative display size of each ZSphere; you may better access individual ZSpheres by adjusting this slider to a lower value. The model's produced mesh and geometry are unaffected by this slider.

DSmooth

The Smoothness Subdivision slider smooths down this 3D object's jagged edges. In this effect, larger values cover a larger portion of the item. This slider does not affect the geometry of the object; it just modifies how the thing appears on the canvas. To smooth the polygons of the object, use the Smooth slider in the Deformation sub-palette.

DRes

The Draw Resolution slider controls how well the current 3D tool draws on the canvas. Polygons will be resized based on the value given in this slider before the object is rendered.

This button just modifies the object's appearance on the canvas; it does not influence the object's real shape. The Divide button in the **Tool > Geometry menu** can be used to divide polygons, which does change the geometry of the object.

Creating Armatures Using ZSpheres

To create an armature with the use of ZSphere, follow the steps below;

- Open the **ZSphere > create a generic human form**.

- Work with symmetry by **pressing X on your keyboard or tapping the symmetry icon**.

- You will notice some dots on either side of the ZSphere which will snap into just one with a green color; this is so because the symmetry is turned on.

- Click **and drag the ZSphere** at both the top and the bottom.

- Design another **ZSphere** at the lower part of the one you are working with which will serve as the leg then create another at the top which will serve as the arm.

- You can pull further such as to make both arms and legs much longer.

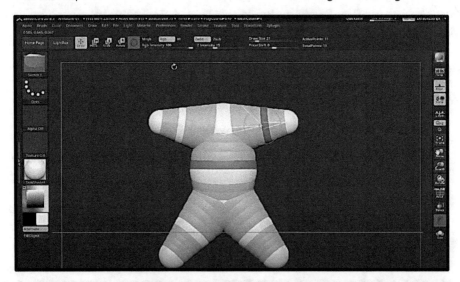

- Move to the center then **create another ZSphere** which will serve as the head. You can then add some more ZSpheres to create the hand, fingers, etc.

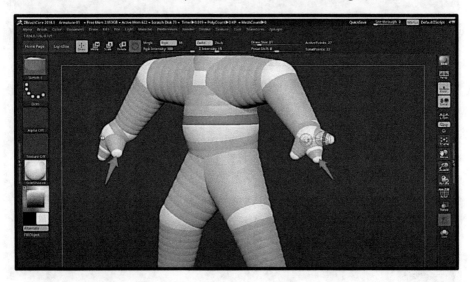

Skinning in ZSpheres

Adaptive Skinning

Adaptive skinning is one of two methods that can be used to skin ZSphere models. It explicitly looks into the structure of the ZSphere model, how child branches grow out of parent branches, and then builds a (typically low-resolution) mesh based on that research. Each ZSphere is (essentially) treated as a cube or rectangular solid when using adaptive skinning, with the Tool: **Adaptive Skin:** The number of polygons along each edge of the cube is determined by the IRes option. Adaptive skinning, which is probably the most often used skinning technique with ZSpheres, gives you a great deal of control over the final topology if you put in the time to prepare ahead.

Note that Adaptive skinning is controlled by making use of the **Tool > Adaptive skin sub-palette**.

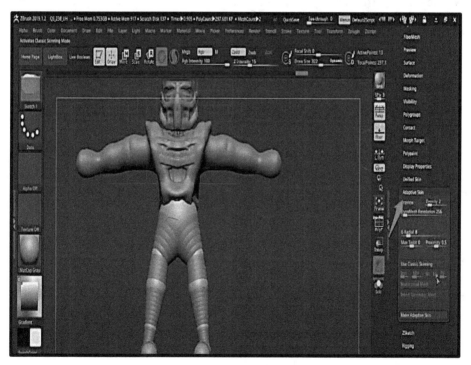

76

Unified Skinning

Zspheres have access to uniform skinning as well. To generate a surface that is subsequently covered with a (often high-resolution) mesh, all ZSpheres are simply combined. Numerous factors determine the mesh's final density, smoothness, and level of adherence to the spheres' outlines. Models with any structure that doesn't require exact topology control or that serves as prototypes for more sophisticated models can be easily created using unified skinning.

Note also that Unified skinning is controlled by the **Tool > Unified Skin sub-palette**.

ZSkteching

With the help of ZSketch, you may create meshes without restriction, allowing you to draw freely in three dimensions and construct your model in any way you see fit. Working with clay strips is a lot like this in that you may add or remove material as needed.

ZSketch can be utilized in three various ways;

- By making use of a **ZSphere skeleton** which will later become an armature for the ZSketch.

- By making use of just one **ZSphere** then design your model in the 3D space.

- By including **a ZSphere** as a sub-tool to any mesh, add sketch mode and draw straight on the other subtool.

Since every approach offers benefits of its own, the approach you select will depend on your goals or just how you want to work.

It's important to keep in mind that ZSketch is built on ZSpheres, so even if you decide not to use the generated ZSphere in a hierarchy, you still need to build ZSphere strips the same way you would a physical model using Clay strips. Steer clear of making simultaneous forward and backward strokes.

It is possible to combine smoothing with the production of these ZSphere strips. ZBrush provides a range of Smooth brushes with different effects on your mesh for sketching.

ZSketch with a ZSphere Structure

The ZSphere skeleton is required for this technique to work. The development of a conventional ZSphere model is the initial stage. The ZSpheres trip through ZSketch will be prepared for application once you have finished creating this building.

- Create **your ZSphere Skeleton**.

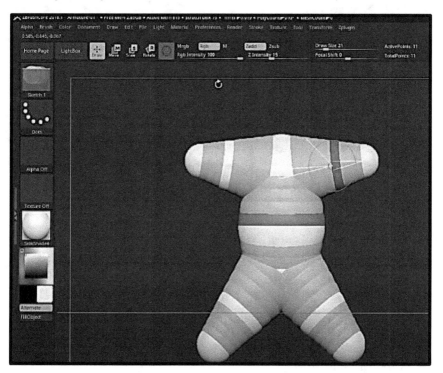

- In the Tool palette, open the **ZSketch menu** and select the **Edit Sketch button**; the color of your ZSphere will then be altered.

- Ensure you have **Edit > Draw mode on**.

- In the brush palette, the traditional sculpting brushes are changed by the **ZSketch tools**. Choose your preferred tools and begin to sculpt.

- Click the **Tool > Unified Skin palette > Preview button**, this will present to you a mesh that is in preview mode. By default, ZBrush is making use of Unified Skin to develop the model.

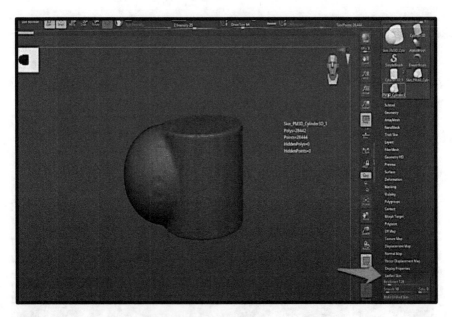

- Press the **A key to return to the Edit Sketch mode** then proceed with your 3D sketch.

- If need be, tap the **Tool > ZSketch > Optimize button**, this will remove the ZSpheres that are not needed such as the ones embedded in the model.

- Repeat these processes until you have finished the model. Press the "A" key to view a preview of your mesh after finishing your design, then select "Make Unified Skin" to create a new mesh that will be added to the Tool Palette.

3D Sketching on a Subtool

This method of sculpting will be applied to every sub-tool that is connected to the ZSphere. Subtools can be given shape and form with great success using this approach. During this process, the sub-tool surface will be used to align the ZSketch strokes. To make the ZSphere fit inside the other subtools, it must first be shrunk. It is important to note that for this method to function, Ghost transparency needs to be off.

- Append just one **ZSphere to any sub-tool**.

- Scale the **ZSphere down** to be on the inside of the sub-tools such that you will be unable to see the appended ZSphere.

- In the Tool palette, open **the ZSketch menu** and select the **Edit Sketch button**; your ZSphere's color will be altered.

- Ensure you have **Edit > Draw mode on**.

- The ZSketch tools replace the conventional sculpting brushes in the brush pallet. Select your favorite tool and start shaping.

- You can examine a mesh in preview mode by using **the "A" key** or by selecting the **Tool > Unified Skin palette > Preview button**. ZBrush generates the model using a Unified Skin by default.

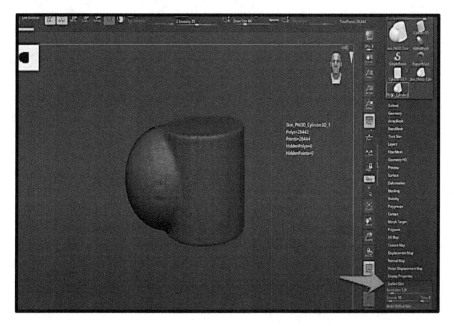

- Press the **A button once more** to return to the **Edit Sketch mode** and continue your 3D sketch.

- If you feel there is a need for it, touch the **Tool > ZSketch > Optimize button**, this will take off ZSpheres that are not needed.

- Take all of these steps over again until your model is completed.

- When done, click on **Make Unified Skin**.

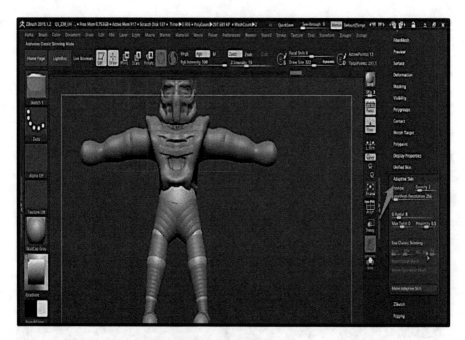

- A new tool will be included in the Tool Palette.

- Add the new tool to the one you previously picked and used for sketching. Where the sketch was placed, the new Unified Skin will go.

Brushes Used in ZSkteching

ZBrush provides a range of brushes for your ZSketch, each of which will provide a distinct effect. Some of them have different settings, but others are nearly the same, as Sketch 1, 2, and 3, which yield the same result at different embedded depths. All the brushes that can be used with ZSketch are explained in detail in the "Brushes" sub-section of Chapter 2.

Rigging Using ZSpheres

The technique of giving a 3D object a skeleton so that it can be posed is known as rigging. This is accomplished in ZBrush utilizing a ZSphere structure.

Below are the step-by-step instructions to be followed for ZSphere rigging

- Draw a **ZSphere** on the screen then go into Edit mode.

- Go to **Tool > Rigging > Select** and choose the mesh that you would like to rig. Ensure the mesh chosen is at a low level of resolution.

- By choosing the ZSphere in the center, you can design multiple ZSpheres. The positions of the ZSpheres are important, but they don't tell you everything about how your skin will turn out. Make sure that the root ZSphere is not in an area where the model exhibits significant curvature, but rather near the model's usual center of gravity. For a standard humanoid, you'll need a ZSphere above the ribcage and a ZSphere below the root for the hip.

- Upon the completion of the skeleton, press **Tool > Rigging > Bind Mesh**. ZBrush is making use of an automatic weighting solution to check your mesh to see if it is correctly weighted.

- Pose your model with the use of the **Rotate or Move. Press A** to have a preview of your low-resolution mesh in that pose.

Note

The angle of the arms should be at least 45 degrees from the body. Otherwise, they risk getting entangled in the spine's ZSpheres.

Press **Bind Mesh** again to unbind the mesh and adjust some of your ZSpheres if the weighting is off. This should turn off the switch and make it non-orange. Occasionally, it is possible to control the mesh deformation by adding more ZSphere chains that connect to certain locations on the object. Press **Bind Mesh** when you're ready to retest the weights.

Previewing your high-resolution details on a posed mesh;

- Create your skeleton as explained above.

- Press **Tool > Rigging > Bind Mesh**.

- Configure **Tool > Adaptive Skin > Density** to the same number as the maximum levels of resolution for the mesh that is being posed.

- Configure DynaMesh Resolution to 0.

- Press Shift and choose the **Tool > Adaptive Skin > Preview button**. This will have the res mesh previewed.

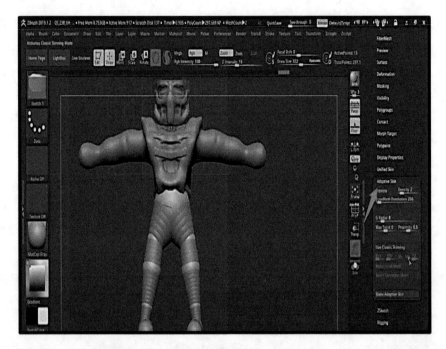

- After pressing **Shift and clicking the Preview button**, you must sculpt a few tiny brush strokes to make this happen each time you press **A**. You won't be able to preview your high-resolution mesh if this step is skipped or reversed.

- You can go ahead to pose your model. When you need to preview the high-resolution mesh simply press **A**.

Self-Evaluation Test

1. With the procedures described in this chapter, create an armature.

2. Skin a Zsphere model.

3. Zsketch a model with the use of a ZSphere structure.

4. Perform 3D Sketching on a sub-tool.

5. Rig with the use of ZSphere.

CHAPTER 6

DYNAMESH, NANOMESH, AND ZREMESHER

Introduction: DynaMesh

DynaMesh is the newest base mesh-generating tool in ZBrush. DynaMesh is ideal for free-form sculpting since it eliminates the need to focus on topological limitations. It is possible to change the general shape of any DynaMesh by pushing or pulling, combining many pieces of geometry into one, or even eliminating geometry in a way similar to what is achievable with Boolean operations. DynaMesh was created to build low and medium-resolution sculpting stages, making it an ideal approach to develop your base mesh before delving further into all of the sophisticated classic ZBrush sculpting and editing tools.

DynaMesh is the newest tool in ZBrush for building foundation meshes. DynaMesh is ideal for free-form sculpting because it does not require the consideration of topological constraints. The general shape of each DynaMesh can be changed by pushing or pulling, integrating many pieces of geometry into one, or even, in a way similar to Boolean operations, eliminating geometry. Using DynaMesh to create your foundation mesh is an excellent idea before you start experimenting with all of the sophisticated old ZBrush sculpting and editing features. DynaMesh was created to create sculpting stages with low and medium resolution.

DynaMesh Area

ZBrush has a mode called DynaMesh that may be applied to primitives. Any existing geometry can also be converted into a DynaMesh, however, bear in mind that DynaMesh works best when creating early in a sculpt, not once extensive detailing has started. The amount of detail in the converted mesh will be set by adjusting the DynaMesh Resolution slider. Any geometry that you convert to a DynaMesh will result in completely new geometry that is evenly distributed throughout the mesh. This removes the pre-existing topological pattern of the original object, which is great for sculpting.

Once you've created a DynaMesh, you can sculpt it with any of ZBrush's sculpting tools. As you make large adjustments to the base shape, polygons may inevitably become warped in some spots.

- Simply **hold CTRL and drag on any open section** of the document at any time throughout this sculpting (and as frequently as you like).

ZBrush will instantly restore a homogenous geometry distribution to your DynaMesh by adding topology. The final product will be a consistent mesh that you can easily sculpt with, even if you stretch geometry to unnatural lengths.

DynaMesh

Initiates the first remeshing and turns on Dynamesh for the selected SubTool. Dynamesh is a model remeshing process that gives your model a whole new topology. The structure is primarily composed of sculpting-tuned, equally distributed quads. whenever you choose (and at any point during the sculpting process).

Groups

When this option is enabled, any DynaMesh with more than one PolyGroup will be split into various pieces. It will also still be kept as one SubTool.

Polish

When this option is enabled, it will apply different ClayPolish settings anytime you make an update to the DynaMesh. This is used to smoothen sharp corners.

Blur

This option adds a smoothing effect to the DynaMesh when the Project is enabled. A low value will give rise to a small amount of smoothness and a high value will ensure the smoothness of all major details on the model.

Project

Upon activation, the DynaMesh is automatically updated with the model's current details. This is useful for creating a DynaMesh from a poly mesh with available data. Remember that the amount of information that can be retained is greatly influenced by the Resolution option.

Resolution

Defines the DynaMesh Resolution, which regulates the model's total polygon density. A low number results in a mesh with low quality and few polygons, whereas a higher number results in a mesh with high resolution and many details but with more polygons. A

DynaMesh with low resolution will update faster than one with high resolution, which would take longer.

Add

By default, all the new elements will be Additive meshes. This simply means that when the remesh operation is ongoing, the inserted items will be combined as a single element with the original DynaMesh.

Sub

When you insert a mesh, ZBrush interprets it as a subtractive (negative) mesh if you hold down the Alt key. This implies that holes will appear after the remesh is complete since the inserted mesh will be eliminated from the original mesh. It's similar to a Boolean subtraction operation at the end, but without the untidy polygons that are usually connected to Booleans.

You can input several meshes and add or subtract them all at once with a single remesh operation. To build multiple combinations at once, you can even blend additive and subtractive meshes.

Create Shell

You can add internal thickness to any DynaMesh by inserting a negative mesh first (Sub).

- When you click the **Create Shell button**, a hole will be created where the Insert brush was used, and an internal thickness will be applied to the entire DynaMesh.

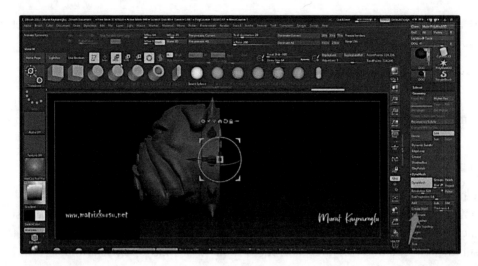

You can change the thickness by moving it inward from the mesh surface using the Thickness slider (below). (To put it another way, it will be contained within the model instead of expanding the surface.) Because it uses less material and hence costs less to print, this tool is perfect for users who want to print their 3D models.

Before you remesh, make sure you move the negative inserted mesh away from the mesh if you don't want a hole when you push the Create Shell button. When the shell is created, it will then be ignored.

Thickness

This option helps with the definition of the thickness of the shell about DynaMesh's resolution.

ZRemesher

The ZRemesher button causes the selected SubTool's visible portions' retopology calculation to open.

The ZRemesher settings are used to modulate the generated retopology, which can significantly change the final mesh.

FreezeGroup

By guaranteeing that the borders remain frozen and joining the edges of the vertices along each PolyGroup border, this mode aids in the independent retopologizing of each PolyGroup.

A model with the same PolyGroups but distinct topologies inside each group will result from this.

Keep Groups

The retopologized model can repeat each of the model's PolyGroups since the retain Group mode maintains its current boundaries.

The Maintain Groups option adjusts the topology while preserving the boundary form, in contrast to the Freeze Groups option, which keeps the topology unchanged at the PolyGroup borders. Consequently, the topological flow becomes better.

Target Polygons Count

The Target Polygons Count slider specifies the number of polygons that ZRemesher should generate. It's called a target for a purpose: sometimes conditions prevent a "bull's eye," and the new topology will have a different number of polygons than what was defined by this slider. This value is heavily influenced by the Adap-tive Size.

If you value precision over polygon optimization, disable ZRemesher's Adaptive Density mode as shown below.

Half

This configures a target that is the same as half of the original polygon count of the model.

Same

This configures the same target such that it matches the model of the original polygon.

Double

In essence, this instructs ZRemesher to create a topology with twice as many polygons as those found in the initial model.

You can combine these parameters with the Adaptive Density mode (described below).

Similarly, when using the Target Polygon Count slider, ZRemesher's output of polygons might not match the quantity entered. To obtain an accurate polygon count, disable the Adaptive Density mode.

Adaptive Size

Since the Adaptive Density mode is enabled by default, ZRemesher prioritizes the Adaptive Size setting over the Target Polygon Count. When this mode is off, ZRemesher's topology computations will be adjusted to give equal weight to your Target Polygon Count number.

That is to say, ZRemesher will typically attempt to reach the target count, but only if doing so does not compromise the topology quality specified by the value selected for the Adaptive Size slider. ZRemesher will calculate a mesh that is incredibly close to the target polygon count when you disable Adaptive Density mode, even if a different count would have resulted in a mesh that is more "perfect".

NanoMesh

A feature of the ZModeler brush, the NanoMesh system takes the process of making use of ZBrush's InsertMesh and MicroMesh features to an entirely new level. The system of the NanoMesh gives room for the population of areas of a model with instanced geometry. These instances can then be altered in real time to generate various scales, offsets, and angles for each instance.

Tutorial

With ZBrush, you may instantly refresh a workable topology across the surface of the Tool or sub-tool that you are now selecting by using the Dynamesh function. As you sculpt, especially with low-resolution models, your polys will get stretched and distorted, which will make more sculpting challenging. This topology is meant to be used as a blank canvas for additional sculpting rather than being sent to rendering or animation tools.

In the early stages of your sculpting, it is crucial since it enables you to quickly pull and stretch a basic sphere into a rough shape for your model before dynamizing it into a practical form.

Dynamesh is not appropriate for modeling details because it is meant to be used early in the design phase to block out huge major shapes. The topology it generates is uneven, with wavy lines and triangles.

Use Z-Remesher after the Dynamesh step to produce a more orderly, consistent topology better suited for detail sculpting.

To use Dynamesh, go to the Geometry tool palette and select the Dynamesh option. To create your new topology, simply click the huge Dynamesh button, and then continue sculpting.

Your polys may distort again over time, so Ctrl + Drag click the background to reproject a dynamesh over the model.

When you've done the base sculpt, make sure to turn off Dynamesh mode!

Merging Subtools

DynaMesh can be used in the merging of two different subtools together into just one mesh. Follow the steps below to do so;

- Let's say you want to add horns to the monster's head and you have a monster head tool and a horn tool. After adding the head tool to the canvas, append the Horn as a new sub-tool. Use the rotate and move scale tools to position the horn.

- Using the head tool, you must first remove any lower Sub-Div Levels. To do this, select the 'Del Lower' button after launching the Geometry panel. Continue using the horn.

- Make sure the horn is listed beneath the head if you have many sub-tools, and then click Merge Down. One tool will be created by combining the two. They will still exhibit a variety of colors even if they have different materials or poly groups, so don't worry.

- Verify that the 'Group' option is not selected next to the Dynamesh button. By doing this, the two meshes will become one. (If the group button was chosen, the edges of both would not come together and would instead be dynameshed as separate meshes.)

Self-Evaluation Test

1. Briefly describe the DynaMesh Area.

2. Create a DynaMesh.

3. Highlight the uses of the NanoMesh.

4. What is the ZRemesher used for?

CHAPTER 7

SHADOWBOX

Introduction: ShadowBox

ShadowBox is a tool for creating various 3D primitives depending on the projection of shadows toward a central volume. Paint the front, side, and bottom shadows of a model using masks onto the specific cubic ShadowBox, and your model will be automatically produced inside it!

The primary goal of ShadowBox is to create any primitive you require in a few strokes, prepared for additional sculpting. It is not meant for finely detailed model creation or sculpting and polishing models. ShadowBox is built on the Remesh and is reliant on resolution. Everybody works: Few polygons and an approximate shape are produced by a low-resolution setting; more polygons and an accurate shape are produced by a high-resolution setting.

Instead of attempting to use ShadowBox at a high resolution to construct very precise masks or intricate base meshes, it is advisable to employ a low-resolution configuration when appropriate, and then much later subdivision the model while sculpting using ZBrush 4's various brushes. Stated differently, create the lowest resolution base mesh possible using the ShadowBox so that it can serve as a foundation for your sculpts.

Creating 3D Objects Using ShadowBox

ShadowBox is a mode of editing. Before you can use ShadowBox, you must first

- Select a **Polymesh3D object from the Tool > Geometry option** above the ClayPolish section.

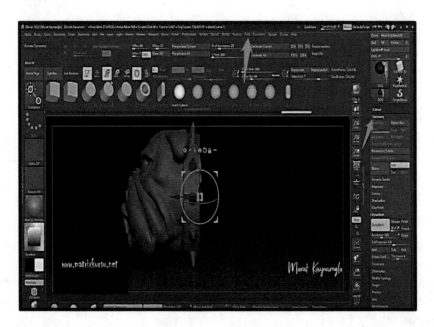

Your object will then become its shadow representation after that: The front, side, and bottom shadows of the loaded item will be projected as masks on the appropriate planes, and as you modify these masks, the mesh will be updated.

During this process, the original mesh will be seen with shadows cast on the three ShadowBox planes. However, this depends on the Resolution selected before starting ShadowBox mode.

If you would like to design a new shape and not commence from one that already exists, you must load one anyway. The fastest solution is the loading of a primitive like the Polymesh 3D and then clearing the converted masks that will be shown. ShadowBox makes use of the mask in the representation of the shadow. If you would like to modify the shadow you ought to use the regular Mask brushes and operators.

Take note of the following;

Your original 3D model will be lost because ShadowBox is in editing mode. Create a clone before turning on ShadowBox if you want to preserve a copy of it.

Loading a ShadowBox project from LightBox is an additional method. Remember that any custom objects that are currently in the Tool palette will be removed when you load a project.

Modifying 3D Objects in the ShadowBox

Upon initializing ShadowBox, you will observe the three operational planes responsible for producing the shadow of the mesh. With ZBrush's masking features, you may start working on them by adding or removing portions of the shadows. To clear the current masks and eliminate everything, hold down the Ctrl+Alt key and drag a selection marquee across the whole ShadowBox. For optimal results, please bear the following in mind before starting to work with ShadowBox:

Change the display mode from perspective to orthogonal (P Hotkey).

- Enable **Ghost transparency** (found on the right shelf or in the Transform palette). This prevents the 3D object from obscuring the projection plane masks.

Before starting work on your project, set the ShadowBox resolution (see below). Don't keep logging in and out of ShadowBox while building your model. ZBrush will reconstruct your geometry after evaluating the projected shadow when you get back to ShadowBox, potentially erasing any modifications you made outside of ShadowBox. When you're ready to work with ShadowBox, begin designing your masks on the Back working plane. To achieve the cleanest mesh, it is preferable to operate in this plane when building a single type of extrusion.

With each new stroke, thin lines will be formed on the three working planes to show the bounding box of your item as it is currently seen in all three viewpoints. This lets you figure out where on the other working planes you may safely keep masking: ZBrush will produce a model in the middle of the box that can be described by the masks that are already there. Only the shared portion is formed if you build a mask on one side and another mask that is not aligned with the preexisting mask on the other side.

Remember that you can delete masked regions by

- Holding **down the ALT key while pressing Ctrl**.

You can also utilize the mask in conjunction with the new Stroke types (Circle, Square, and Curve) or the new masking brushes (Mask Rectangle, Mask Circle, etc.). To get sharp lines for hard-edged meshes, use the LazyMouse and Backtrack capabilities. When you're finished with ShadowBox, simply turn off the ShadowBox switch. Your new base mesh is now complete and ready for sculpting with all of the ZBrush brushes.

Symmetry in the ShadowBox

ShadowBox works well with Symmetry, axis-based symmetry, and the Radial (R) option selected. If your symmetry is off-axis, be sure to turn on the Local Symmetry option in the Transform panel.

Attributes of the ShadowBox With Subtools

While ShadowBox can load a ShadowBox model as a SubTool or change a SubTool, it cannot communicate directly with SubTools. You can see all of the SubTools that are presented in ShadowBox, but you won't be able to edit them if you have Ghost Transparency mode on. This is a straightforward process that uses other SubTools as a comparison to create basic meshes or props.

Making use of references on working planes

The standard 3D planes with UVs are the ShadowBox working planes. This implies that the image can be used as a reference because you can load a texture and apply it straight on the planes. Using PolyPaint to paint directly on the planes is an additional choice. Either the traditional PolyPainting technique or SpotLight can be used to achieve this.

Using Alphas in ShadowBox

You must generate the alpha to match ShadowBox's UV mapping. To do so, open the ShadowBox128 project in Lightbox,

- Navigate to the **Tool >Texture Map menu**, and select **Clone Txtr.** This copies the texture map to the Texture palette, from whence it can be exported.

- Loathe **ShadowBox texture map** into the editor of your image.

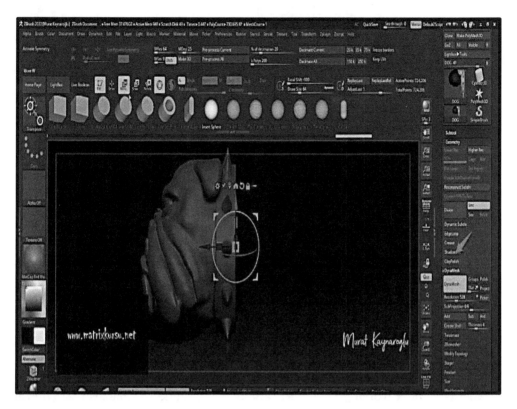

- Make use of the map as a guide for the creation of your alpha.

- Load the **alpha into ZBrush**.

- Upon the loading of ShadowBox, erase any masking by pressing **Ctrl + click + dragging the background of the canvas**.

- With your alpha chosen in the Alpha palette, tap **Tool > Masking > Mask By Alpha**.

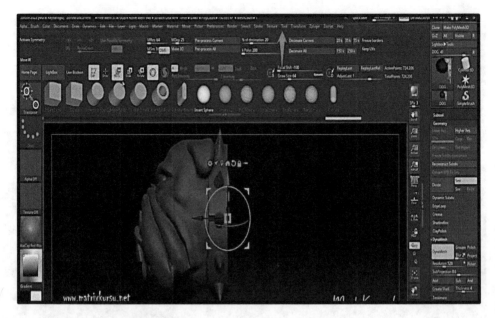

- **Ctrl + click in ShadowBox** to ensure it gets updated.

Hiding working planes

Each ShadowBox working plane has various polygroups. This means that you can conceal any or all working planes at any time by

- Pressing **Ctrl + Shift + clicking on the preferred plane**.

You can focus on one plane at a time using this method, and then return one or both of the other planes as a single ShadowBox.

To unfold ShadowBox for flat painting, use

- The new **Unwrap UV function is in the Tool > UV Map menu**.

ZBrush will produce a mesh where the masking on your three planes joins when you click Unwrap UV again.

The major sculpting points for ShadowBox are highlighted below;

Rather than creating intricately detailed models, ShadowBox is meant to create foundation meshes. Rather than attempting to build your object entirely with ShadowBox, it is often far preferable to construct a rough with few polygons, then divide and shape it with traditional tools.

If holes need to be made, make sure they are made in ShadowBox by using Ctrl + Alt to clean a portion of the mask.

Keep in mind to use the new masking Brushes to generate precise shadows. These can be coupled with the new stroke functions to make perfect circles and other shapes.

ShadowBox works well with Symmetry, based on an axis, or with the Radial (R) option selected. If your symmetry is off-axis, be sure you enable the Local Symmetry option in the Transform panel.

Tutorial

Prototyping Models with a Shadowbox

To begin, in ZBrush, go to **Geometry > Shadowbox**. This will display a three-planed, isometric cube. This is your model's bounding box; by default, Shadowbox forms a cube that you can shape any way you see fit. ZBrush is essentially told what information to generate when you draw masks on any of these planes. Information will be created starting from one side of the mask and continuing until information on another plane is completely hidden. Once your model is to your satisfaction, just click Shadowbox once more, and you can start sculpting and altering your new base mesh. Since ZBrush will recalculate the model Shadowbox creates, reentering Shadowbox will distort certain information. Therefore, if you have finer details and don't want to lose them, duplicate your model.

Shadowbox Resolution

You might need to work at a higher resolution if you find that the data in your Shadowbox appears pixelated. Low-resolution information may cause the final model to appear cluttered since the mask information, which determines the final model, will be drawing each pixel rather than gentle curves. Before launching Shadowbox, raise the resolution in the Remesh section to any value more than the default 128.

To achieve smoother effects with Shadowbox, increase the resolution. If you only need to build a rough model that you will split apart and sculpt regularly, leave it at default or reduce it for a lighter base mesh.

Boost your resolution in Shadowbox for smoother effects. Keep the default or decrease it for a lighter base mesh if you only need to construct a preliminary model that you will later subdivide and sculpt regularly.

Self-Evaluation Test

1. Create a 3D object with the use of Shadowbox.

2. Modify the 3D object you have created with the use of Shadowbox.

3. Highlight some attributes of the Shadowbox.

CHAPTER 8

MATERIALS IN ZBRUSH

Introduction: Materials in ZBrush

The appearance of each surface in ZBrush is influenced by various factors, including its base color, texture image (if it has one), lighting that falls on the surface, and material. The material alters how light interacts with the surface, causing it to appear glossy, rough, reflecting, metallic, or transparent. In ZBrush, there are various preset materials to allow you control over a scene. Furthermore, each substance can be changed to produce new materials.

You can create your unique materials or obtain them from places like ZBrushCentral, the Pixologic MatCap Library, and others.

By saving a custom material to the ZStartup/Materials folder, you can ensure that it is available every time ZBrush starts. But, don't overburden this folder, since this may have an impact on ZBrush's performance - keep it to a maximum of 25 materials.

MatCap Materials

Image maps are used in MatCap materials to replicate the effects of lighting on various types of surfaces. Because the lighting is fixed by the picture map, alterations made in the Light palette have no effect. MatCap is an abbreviation for material capture, and the MatCap tool allows you to quickly develop your own MatCap materials that accurately imitate real-world surfaces.

Standard Materials

The BasicMaterial serves as the foundation for the majority of the common materials, such as Toy Plastic, Double, Shader material, TriShader materials, and QuadShader materials.

These materials have all of the same properties as Basic materials, but they have one, two, three, or four shader channels.

Material Palette

The Material palette has a library of materials that you can choose from. Each material has modifiers that give room for interaction with light in a very unique manner. As against some other palettes, materials are usually not added to, or removed from this palette. They can however be replaced with materials loaded from disk files.

The huge material thumbnail serves as a picker; click inside this window and move to the canvas to choose the material. Furthermore, ZBrush remembers all materials utilized in the document and saves them along with the project, whether customized or not. When you edit or load a material here, it affects all painted elements on the canvas that use that material.

Load

The Load Material button helps with the replacement of the chosen material with a saved one.

Save

The Save Material button helps with saving the chosen material to a disk file.

LightBox Materials

Lightbox is simply a browser that can show the content of folders that are on your hard drive.

Lightbox will display the contents of the following folders in the ZBrush root folder: Documents, Tool, Brushes, Material, Alphas, Textures, ZScript, and Other.

Save your stuff at any moment by utilizing the default ZBrush Save/Export buttons for each item: **Brush > Save as, Texture > Export**, and so on. Light Box allows you to save your items in your folders and explore them.

Lightbox allows you to save shortcuts. If you have an external hard drive,

- You can create a shortcut in the **ZBrush 4R5 >ZTools** folder to ensure that it is always available when you use Light Box.

If there will be a need for you to gain access to your folders in the Other tab all you have to do is save all of your Texture, Alphas, etc in the **ZBrush > ZExport import folder**. With this, anytime you click on the other tab, all of your folders will be there. If you would like to open an element, click on such element twice. If it is a 3D model /ZTool, it will instantly be loaded. If it's material, it will be loaded and chosen.

- Click **twice on the textures or alphas** will have them loaded into the Spotlight.
- If you would like to load a file into the Texture or Alpha palette, hold **Shift** and click twice.
- Holding **Alt and clicking twice** will open an image in its default editor, or in the case of web images, open the original web page in your browser.

- Alphas should be single-channel grayscale files, either 16bit or 8bit. Three-channel (RGB) grayscale photos will be loaded into the Texture palette.
- Use the PSD file format if possible. Only TIF files made by ZBrush will be loaded.

Lightbox Navigation

Lightbox has numerous options for navigating and displaying its content:

Click on one of the following category titles at the top to display and view its content: **ZBrush, Documents, Tool, Brush, Material, Script, and Miscellaneous. These are links to ZBrush's default folders**.

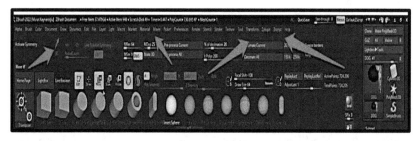

- To switch from one category to another, click **the left or right arrow** on the right of these default folders.
- To move up in the hard disk hierarchy, click **the left folder with the up arrow**.
- To access these folders, click on the other folder icons.
- Choose **one, two, three, or four lines of icons to display** in the upper right corner.
- To modify the size of the content preview, **click and drag on the inner edge (nearest the center of the Canvas) of the Lightbox window**.
- To shift the Lightbox material to the left or right, click and drag in the content, and then click on the preview icon.

Lightbox Preferences

The **Preference > Lightbox sub-palette** contains the Lightbox configurations which include functions it uses in the opening of the ZBrush startup. Uncheck the Open At Launch option to ensure the Lightbox closes when the ZBrush is being launched.

You can customize the visual appearance of Lightbox as well as the number of threads utilized to create previews of the presented content using several parameters. Additional threads will result in a faster thumbnail display.

Save As Startup Material

By saving a custom material to the ZStartup/Materials folder, you can ensure that it is available every time ZBrush starts. But, don't overburden this folder, since this may have an impact on ZBrush's performance - keep it to a maximum of 25 materials.

Show Used

The Show Used button helps with the examination of all the various materials utilized in the document and shows their corresponding icons in this palette.

CopyMat / PasteMat

Enables you to copy one content and paste it into another to replace it. You can use this if you wish to update the substituted material everywhere it appears in the scene. It's also useful for making a clone of a starting material so you can change it without affecting the original.

WaxModfiers

The **Material > WaxModifiers sub-palette** offers various options for the creation of a wax effect for the chosen material. This effect is visually close to a Sub Surface Scattering effect but also needs less effort to achieve a very good result. Another advantage of Wax over SSS is that the ZBrush Preview render may show this effect as you sculpt in real time.

Just enable Wax Preview in the **Render > Render Properties menu**. The wax effect can then be adjusted using the options in the Render > Preview Wax menu, just like the BPR Wax shader, which is only used for full BPR renders.

Strength

The strength slider indicates the amount of wax effect that should be added to the model. A high value will ensure the model shows that it is very waxy while a much smaller value will give rise to a subtle SSS-like effect.

Spec

The Specular Highlight slider controls how much the wax substance affects your model's specularity. It should be noted that MatCap lacks a specular component. As a result, if a MatCap is utilized, the specular values in the Wax modifiers have no effect. The standard materials, on the other hand, contain a specular component that is modified by the specular value in the Wax Modifiers.

Fresnel

The slider of this unique feature indicates if the wax effect will be added on the surface of the model that is facing the camera or if it will be on the surfaces of the model angled off the camera. A negative value will adversely affect the front of the surface while a positive value will affect the sides of the surface.

Exponent

The Exponent slider controls how quickly the wax effect's Fresnel falloff is applied to the surface. In other words, the degree to which a modification in surface angle affects the wax.

Radius

The slider of the radius helps with the indication of just how far the wax effect spreads out from the places where other settings determine it should be sort of waxy.

A low value will bring about a reduction of the area of the wax while a high value will add more to the amount of wax rendered across the surface of the model.

Temperature

The Temperature slider influences the wax temperature, much to the light temperature in photography. A negative number tints the wax cold (blue), while a positive value tints it hot (red).

Modifiers

The **Material > Modifiers sub-palette**

Offers a plethora of options for customizing the effects of the selected material. The majority of impacts govern how the material interacts with light. Certain materials are arranged with distinct sets of modifiers within numerous Shaders; to access them, click the active Shader buttons. When rendering the material, all shaders and their effects are blended.

CopySH

This button copies a single shader channel (S1, S2, S3, or S4) and pastes it into another shader channel in the same or a different material. You cannot paste into a nonactive channel, but you may make whatever combination of shader channels you like by copying and pasting a material with all four channels activated and then pasting it into the copy.

PasteSH

Paste Shader which is a previously copied shader. You cannot paste into a channel that is not active, but by copying and pasting materials with all four channels active, and then pasting into the copy option, you can design any combination of shader channels you like.

Ambient

The Ambient slider controls the amount of ambient light rendered by this material shader. Ambient light is unshaded and has no source; an ambient value of 100 renders the effects of this shader in full, unshaded color.

Diffuse

The Diffuse slider controls how much of the overall darkening of the material is generated by light sources. The Diffuse slider's impact makes the material brightest when the object directly meets a light, blending the color of the object with the color of the light.

Specular

The Specular slider controls the shininess of this shader by adjusting the intensity of 'hot spots' where light sources strike the object's surface. Typically, the specular property renders the colors of the light sources at the set intensity, taking precedence over the underlying color of the object. The Metallicity and Colorize Specular sliders below can be used to modify this color. The 'hot spots' on the object's surface do not directly face the light sources, but rather a point halfway between both the light sources and you, the viewer.

Transparency

The slider of the transparency helps with the determination of the transparency of this shader. There are some rules for the creation of transparent materials. First, flattened layers ought to be turned off to allow for transparent effects. Second, items that are on the same layers as the transparent material are not shown. The transparency slider can be configured to either a positive or negative value. If it is positive, transparency is then dependent on whether the surface faces you the viewer, or if it faces a right angle away from you. If it is negative, transparency will be based on the color of the object or the texture lightness which also includes any Noise if it has been defined in this material.

Reflectivity

This slider helps to check the internal reflectivity of this shader. The effect of this slider is to allow areas of the surface to show a specified texture, chosen by the material texture picker. The reflectivity slider can be configured to a positive or negative value. Similar to the transparency slider, positive values determine the reflection depending on whether the surface is facing the viewer, or facing a right angle away from you. Negative values check for the reflection depending on the color of the object or texture lightness which includes any noise if it is defined in this material.

Metallicity

The Metallicity slider influences the color of the Specular light characteristic. Typically, specular light is displayed with the colors of the light sources. This slider allows Specular light to be displayed with the existing object color, making the material seem more metallic. The value of this slider influences how much of the color mixes with the light color; if it is set to 100%, Specular light will become the underlying color at its sharpest.

Noise

The Noise slider gives the material a mottled appearance by generating a random pattern of lights and darks. The Noise slider can be configured to either positive or negative values, resulting in two distinct noise effects.

Env. Reflection

The Environmental Reflection slider controls the shader's environmental reflection. Unlike the Reflectivity characteristic, this impact is applied uniformly across the entire surface. Environmental Reflection is only visible when Best Render or BPR mode is selected. You can specify several different types of environmental attributes in the Render palette, which is mirrored in any material with this slider set higher than 0. There are three types of reflected environments: color alone, selected texture, and the entire canvas (applied as a complete picture, so items may appear to be reflecting themselves).

Apply Different Materials to a Subtool

You can apply various materials to diverse Subtools in ZBrush with the simple steps below;

- Choose a **preferred SubTool**.
- To open the material selector, click **the Material icon**. The Material icon is located on the interface's left side, directly above the color picker. Click **to select a preferred material from the material picker's possibilities**.
- You can then fill in the sub-tool. Note that it is however possible to fill the sub-tool with color from the material only (if RGB alone is chosen). To guarantee the next operation will fill the sub-tool with the material and the color, choose Mrgb.
- Choose the Color menu to open the **Color palette > choose a preferred color**

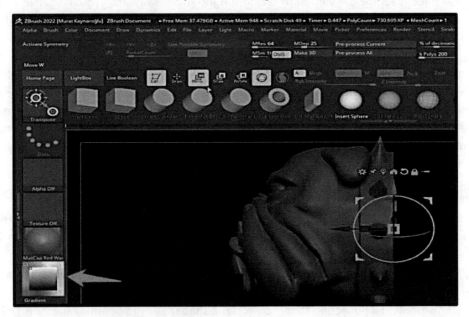

In the **color picker > choose the Fill object option**. The material and color shown ought to be added to the active SubTool.

You can choose another preferred **SubTool using Tool > SubTool** then take the whole process again.

Self-Evaluation Test

1. Make use of Matcap materials and Standard materials in sculpting a model.

2. List 5 features of the material palette.
3. Apply different materials to your model.

CHAPTER 9

TEXTURING IN ZBRUSH

Introduction: Textures in ZBrush

Import

The import button loads a texture from a file that has been saved. ZBrush recognizes several standard image formats for both import and export.

Export

The export button helps to protect the current texture of an image file. ZBrush recognizes some standard image formats for both import and export.

Clone

Employ the use of the clone texture button to design a copy of the chosen texture. This button is disabled when Texture Off is chosen.

MakeAlpha

The MakeAlpha button includes the chosen texture to the Alpha palette, where it is then converted to a grayscale image.

FillLayer

Cd

The **Clear Depth button** affects the Crop and Fill buttons. All depth information is removed from the canvas when it is filled with the current texture and the button is pressed. The canvas's empty regions—those behind the clipping plane—won't display to change if this button is left unpressed. The Fill button in the Layer palette and the Fill Layer button in the Color palette are similarly impacted by this button.

CropAndFill

The document was filled and cropped to the width and height of the chosen texture using the Crop and Fill Document option. ZBrush asks you to confirm this operation first because it cannot be undone.

GrabDoc

The Texture palette now includes a snapshot of the entire canvas thanks to the Grab Texture from Document button. This new texture will have the same height and width as the document.

Texture Palette

There are many different types of patterns and images in the Texture palette. Textures can be applied to the surface of a 3D object or utilized as a painting medium. You can import textures from disk files or use the MRGBZGrabber Tool to grab them directly off the canvas to add them to this palette. Each Texture can also be exported in several formats as an image file.

Spotlight

Spotlight v2.0 is a projection texturing method that enables you to create your source texture directly in ZBrush before painting it on your object in 3D. It's similar to the ZBrush Stencil tool in certain aspects.

Your textures must first be loaded into the Light Box, Texture palette, or Alpha palette. Then, you can utilize the spotlight to modify their hue to match another texture, fill colors, clone portions of the texture, nudge them to match any sculpture, and much more. An interface that is small in size but packed with power. Your ability to paint will soar! With Spotlight v1.0, artists may use PolyPaint to project any texture's color information onto a sculpted surface. Using the same textures for sculptural features on any model's surface also helped. Spotlight v2.0 adds the ability to convert any grayscale image (alpha) into a 3D model while maintaining all of the features of the original version. The original images can be altered or combined using Boolean-style addition or subtraction to create more intricate 3D patterns. The model in this system can be used as a basis for sculpture, or combined with our Live Boolean system to create intricate artwork.

Rotate

You can click on and move the rotate icon in a clockwise and also counter-clockwise manner to rotate an image. When you hold the shift key while rotating you can snap your rotation to the notches displayed on the inner part of the SpotLight dial.

Scale

To scale a picture, click on it and move it in both clockwise and counterclockwise directions using the rotate icon. The width and height will be proportionate by default. You can use the scale to scale the image in a non-proportional way while still holding down the CTRL key.

Opacity

To increase or decrease the opacity of all photos loaded within SpotLight,

- **Click and drag the opacity icon** in both a clockwise and counterclockwise manner.

How much of the image gets painted or carved onto your model is unaffected by the level of opacity you apply to your photos. Instead, this is controlled by the RGB Intensity and Z Intensity sliders. To lessen the impact of an image, use the Fade tool rather than the Intensity settings.

Background Opacity

When you are working with a single image over another, making adjustments to the background opacity will modify the opacity of the back image with which you will be able to configure the opacity to suit your working method.

Fade

As you paint and/or sculpt the photos into your model in Spotlight, you can have layers of images on top of each other to mix and combine the images. The use of fade can help manage how much of an impact an individual image will have inside a stack of images.

By default, the Fade value of spotlight photos is set to 100%, meaning that no fading has been done. The image darkens as the Fade amount is decreased. This implies that when you paint or sculpt, it will blend in with the image underneath if you place it on top of another image.

To raise or reduce the degree of fading applied to an image,

- **Click and drag the Fade symbol** in both a clockwise and counterclockwise direction.

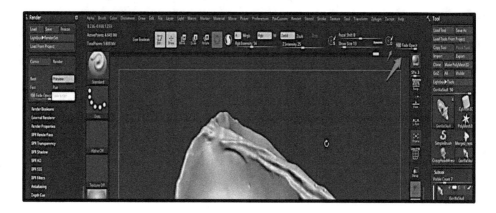

Quick Select

When this option is enabled, its mode will then replace the chosen alpha or texture with the next option chosen. The chosen image will replace the former one, making use of the exact location, scale, and orientation.

Tile Proportional

Upon selecting a texture, the actual pixel size will be shown in the upper left corner of the ZBrush interface. The largest pixel texture will be identified by remaining at the top of the tie and will also appear larger visually. Clicking this option will assist in tiling the textures on the left side of the document space based on each texture's pixel size.

Tile Selected

When you click on this option it will keep the chosen image large but tile every other texture beneath the chosen texture at a much smaller size.

Tile Unified

When you choose this option, it will tile all textures to the same size and also position them on the left side of the document space.

Front

When you click on this icon, the active image will be brought to the front of all the other images loaded into Spotlight.

Back

When you click on this icon, you will send the images that are active to the back of all the other images that have been loaded into the Spotlight.

Delete

Selecting this icon will cause the Spotlight interface's active image to disappear. Because the active images have been removed, all remaining images will be controlled by the spotlight dial in terms of movement, rotation, and scale until a new active image is displayed.

Duplicate

When you click the Duplicate icon, the active image in the SpotLight interface is duplicated.

Union

By applying Boolean-style operations to SpotLight alphas, the Union function enables you to employ basic shapes to create more intricate ones. The way the Union mode operates is by appending or removing alpha from another one that is nested below the current one. The relative locations of the alphas kept in SpotLight are shown graphically via the alpha bounding box.

By default, Alphas are simply combined. Modifiers enable you to alter the outcome:

Utilizing union with;

- **Alt pressed**: The selected alpha will be subtracted from the current alpha, which is situated beneath it. This alpha needs to connect with another alpha for the subtraction to be completed.

- **Alt + Shift pressed**: the alpha in use will perform an intersection with the alpha existing that can be found beneath the chosen one.

Though it was created to work with alphas, Union can also be utilized with textures.

Snapshot 3D

Depending on the modifier key held while using this function, the Snapshot function turns the selected alpha into a 3D model, either as a new SubTool or as an extension to an existing SubTool.

Making use of SnapShot with;

- **Alt Pressed**: Subtractive mode will be applied to the resulting SubTool. If Live Boolean is enabled, the 3D model will be hidden and subtracted from current SubTools.

- **Alt + Shift pressed**: The SubTool that results will be in Intersection mode. When Live Boolean is enabled, just the intersecting portion of the 3D model is revealed.

- **Shift pressed**: The produced mesh will be included with the current sub-tool as against having to create another one.

Frame

By clicking and dragging the mouse above the Frame symbol, this function will create an outline depending on the alpha or picture limits. The function only takes into account the white pixels in an image when it is selected. Other colors will disappear.

Making use of Frame with;

- **Shift key pressed**: The frame action will be modified into an Expand function, making the alpha grow in an outward manner.

- **Alt key pressed**: The frame action will be modified to a Shrink function, making the alpha pull inwardly.

Fil H- Mirror H

This function performs a horizontal flip of the chosen alpha or texture.

Modifiers change this;

- **Shift key pressed**: Depending on whether you employ horizontal or vertical movement, the mirror will be performed from left to right or top to bottom.

- **Alt key pressed**: Depending on whether you employ the horizontal or vertical movement, the mirror will be executed from right to left or bottom to top.

Flip V - Mirror V

This function performs a vertical flip of the chosen alpha or texture.

Modifiers change this;

- **Shift key pressed:** the mirror will be performed from left to right or from top to bottom based on whether you are making use of the horizontal or vertical action.

- **Alt key pressed**: the mirror will be performed from right to left or from bottom to top based on whether you are making use of the horizontal or vertical action.

The center of the mirror is configured by the center location of the spotlight dial.

Extend H

Your texture or alpha can be stretched or contracted along the horizontal axis using the Extend H function. By duplicating the pixels in the SpotLight Dial's center, it achieves this.

The expansion or shrinking position is represented by the two red and green axes in the center of the SpotLight Dial. It is essential to click and drag the dial to put it correctly before proceeding.

No matter where the SpotLight Dial is positioned, pressing the Extend key while holding down the Shift key will cause the action to be initiated from the texture's or alpha's center.

Extend V

Your texture or alpha can be stretched or contracted along the vertical axis using the Extend V function. By duplicating the pixels in the SpotLight Dial's center, it achieves this.

The expansion or shrinking position is represented by the two red and green axes in the center of the SpotLight Dial. It is essential to click and drag the dial to put it correctly before proceeding.

The **Extend key with the Shift key** pressed will conduct the action from the texture or alpha's center, irrespective of where the SpotLight Dial is positioned.

Tile H

This function will duplicate the alpha or texture along the horizontal axis, within the bounding box of the chosen image. The more the Tile value is increased, the more your image will shrink so it allows it to be duplicated in line with the tile axis.

When you make use of Tile with the Shift key pressed, it will enable the function to operate on both the vertical and horizontal axis simultaneously while ensuring the proportions are well preserved.

Tile V

Within the bounding box of the chosen image, the Tile V function replicates the texture or alpha along the vertical axis. Your image will be smaller the higher the Tile value so that it can be copied along the tile axis.

Holding down the Shift key while using Tile causes the function to act simultaneously on the vertical and horizontal axes, maintaining the proportions.

Clone

The Clone brush enables you to clone various parts of an image onto itself or to some other images that have been loaded in the spotlight.

Choose the Clone icon from the Spotlight dial to start using the Clone brush. The RGB intensity slider modifies the Clone brush's strength. Underneath the orange circle on the spotlight dial is the center of the source region that will be replicated. After choosing the Clone brush, you may start cloning from the source position by painting any image in SpotLight. In Spotlight, to clone a different texture onto a different image,

- **Click on the image you want to edit, then click on the Clone Icon, then use the orange circle to move the SpotLight dial** over the other texture you want to clone from (do not click on the other texture as this will select it), then return the brush to the texture you want to edit and paint.

With the Restore brush, you can restore a copied portion of your image. You will not be able to change the SpotLight dial by clicking on a picture when in brush mode. To move the SpotLight dial around the canvas, instead, **click and drag within the orange circle** at the center of the dial.

To quit this brush mode, click the **Clone icon again**.

Smudge

Spotlight allows you to smudge specific sections of the photographs you've loaded by using the Smudge brush. Choose the Smudge icon from the SpotLight dial to utilize the Smudge brush.

The RGB Intensity slider determines how strong the Smudge brush is. In the brush mode, the Smudge brush will be selected. Now, you can click and paint on any imported photo in SpotLight to blur it. You may also use the smudge brush to simultaneously blur an entire image. Make sure the right image is covered by the orange circle located in the center of the SpotLight dial before attempting to blur it.

To make a box blur, **click and drag the Smudge symbol clockwise the whole length of the SpotLight dial.**

To add extra radial blur, **click and drag the Smudge symbol clockwise for a tiny section of the SpotLight dial before releasing**. Once the proper amount of blur is achieved, keep using this technique. You may fix sections of your blurry or smudged photos with the Restore brush. When in brush mode, clicking on an image will not allow you to adjust the SpotLight dial. Instead, click and drag inside the orange circle located in the center of the SpotLight dial to move it about the canvas. To exit this brush mode, press the **Smudge symbol once more**.

Contrast

You can use the Contrast brush to change the contrast of the pictures you've loaded into SpotLight.

Click on the Contrast icon in the SpotLight dial to activate the Contrast brush.

The RGB Intensity slider influences the power of the Contrast brush. The contrast brush will be chosen in brush mode. To begin altering the contrast,

- **Click and paint on any picture loaded within Spotlight**.

To minimize contrast in an image, **hold down the Alt key while using the Contrast brush**.

Alternatively, you can use the Contrast brush to instantly adjust the contrast of a whole image. To begin, move the orange circle in the SpotLight dial's center over the image you want to adjust the contrast for. **Click and drag the Contrast icon clockwise** to improve the contrast of an entire image. To reduce contrast for a full image, **click and drag the Contrast icon counterclockwise**.

You can adjust the contrast in areas of your image that have been increased or decreased by using the Restore brush. When in brush mode, you will not be able to adjust the SpotLight dial by clicking on an image. Instead, click and drag inside the orange circle located in the center of the SpotLight dial to move it about the canvas. To exit this brush mode, select the **Contrast symbol once more.**

Saturation

The Saturation brush permits you to add or remove saturation from areas of photos in SpotLight. Click **on the Saturation icon in the SpotLight dial** to activate the Saturation brush. The RGB Intensity slider influences the Saturation brush's strength.

The saturation brush will be chosen in the brush mode. At this point, you may start applying saturation to any image loaded in SpotLight by clicking and painting on it.

To remove saturation from an image, **hold down the Alt key while using the Saturation brush**.

You can also use the saturation brush to instantly add or subtract saturation from an entire image. Now, align the image you want to add or remove saturation from with the orange circle in the center of the SpotLight dial.

To add saturation to a whole image, click and drag the saturation sign in a clockwise direction. To reduce saturation in an image, click and drag the saturation symbol in a counterclockwise direction. You can restore a section of an image that has had saturation added or subtracted with the Restore brush.

You are not going to be able to change the SpotLight dial by clicking on a picture when in brush mode. To move the SpotLight dial around the canvas, instead, **click and drag within the orange circle at the center of the dial**. Select the Saturation symbol again to quit this brush mode.

Hue

The Hue brush lets you modify the hue of photographs you've loaded into SpotLight. To use the Hue brush, select **the Hue icon from the SpotLight dial**.

The RGB Intensity slider influences the saturation brush's power. The Hue brush will be chosen when you are in brush mode. At this point, you can begin adjusting the hue of any image imported in SpotLight by clicking and painting on it. To modify the hue of a whole image, **click and drag the Hue symbol clockwise**.

You can add or remove Hue from a section of your image and then use the Restore brush to bring it back.

When in brush mode, clicking on an image will not allow you to adjust the SpotLight dial. Instead, click and drag inside the orange circle located in the center of the SpotLight dial to move it about the canvas. To exit this brush mode, select the Saturation symbol once more.

Intensity

The Intensity brush lets you adjust the intensity of photos you've loaded into SpotLight. Click on the Intensity icon in the SpotLight dial to activate the Intensity brush. The RGB Intensity slider influences the strength of the Intensity brush. You will be in brush mode while the Intensity brush is selected. At this point, you can begin increasing Intensity by clicking and painting on any image loaded into SpotLight.

Holding down the Alt key while using the Intensity brush can lessen the intensity of an image. (Remember that if you reduce a region of your image's intensity to black, that area will turn transparent.) The Intensity brush can also be used to instantly alter the intensity of a whole image. To accomplish this, make sure the orange circle in the center of the SpotLight slider is over the image you wish to increase or subtract intensity from.

To increase the intensity of a whole image, click and drag the Intensity sign in a clockwise direction. To remove intensity from a whole image, click and drag the intensity indicator in a counterclockwise direction.

An image turns transparent when its overall intensity reaches absolute black. You may make sections of your image that you have increased or lowered appear again by using the Restore brush.

When in brush mode, clicking on an image will not allow you to adjust the SpotLight dial. Instead, click and drag inside the orange circle located in the center of the SpotLight dial to move it about the canvas. To dismiss this brush mode, **click the Intensity icon a second time.**

Paint

You can use the Paintbrush to paint color strokes, fill a piece of a picture, or fill the full image with a specific color.

Click the Paint icon in the SpotLight dials to activate the Paintbrush.

- **Painting a color stroke**: When the Paintbrush is selected, you are now in brush mode. Now, Spotlight allows you to paint on any image. The primary color that will be painted will be chosen based on the color palette. Using the Alt key, you can change while painting to the secondary color chosen via the Color palette.

The RGB Intensity slider influences the intensity of the color that is painted.

- **Filling an image with color**: You can fill an image with either the primary or secondary color all at once.

To fill the full image, make sure the orange circle in the center of the SpotLight dial is over the correct image.

Click and drag the paint icon clockwise to fill an image with the main color.

To add the secondary color to an image, click and drag the paint icon counterclockwise.

Texturing with Spotlight

The innovative spotlight painting system enables image editing in ZBrush and then enables the projection of images to the surface of the model with the use of intuitive sculpting and painting brushes.

Spotlight is more than simply a tool for texturing. Accurate positioning, layering, and editing are possible with imported photos. To create a completely new image, adjust the hue and intensity, color match some other photos, clone, tile, and color key. You can project color onto any area of your model by using these images. Apply skin tone, tattoos, and other effects to both sides of a face or character simultaneously by using symmetry! Using Spotlight is nearly absurdly simple. Everything you require is easily accessible, and precise control is made possible by real-time feedback. Your ability to fully express your artistic abilities will be enhanced by your comprehension of its various features.

Polypainting

Polypainting gives room for the painting on the surface of a model without the need to first assign a texture map. A texture map can be designed at a much later time, and the surface painted can also be sent to the map. Polypainting provides significant advantages against the standard workflow.

It is not necessary to choose the texture map's resolution in advance of the event. In essence, this is helpful if you appear to require more information on a subject than you had previously believed. You have the option to transfer the current surface painting to a new, much larger map without having to start from scratch when creating a larger texture map. In a similar vein, UV unwrapping is not required before planning. Build a new unwrapping and move the surface painting to it if the first one isn't suitable. To work with more polygons and free up system resources, remove UVs from your model!

Take into consideration a texture map with a resolution of 2048 by 2048 to get an idea of how poly painting operates. In total, it features a little over 4 million pixels. When dealing with a 4 million polygon model, surface painting with just a consistent color applied to each polygon yields the same amount of information as a 4 million pixel texture map. (In actuality, a little bit more, since texture maps usually have large blank areas.) Because of this, poly painting allows you to paint directly on the polygons of the model and then, after the painting is complete, transfer that detail to a texture map.

Tutorial 1

Texture maps

To texture the clothes, you will need to build UVs so that texture maps can be applied. Pick an image of a real fabric you like, preferably one with no seams because you don't want random seams where there shouldn't be any.

Use the UVMaster plug-in - go to **ZPlugin > UVMaster and select Work on Clone**; ZBrush will create a clone of the geometry for you to work with. ZBrush will build the UVs for that geometry with the clone; go to **Tool > UV Map > Morph UV** to unwrap your selection into UV layout. Navigate to **Tool > Texture Map > and select your desired fabric image by clicking on the thumbnail to open an import box**. Once your image has been imported, click Texture On in the same window to instantly see the texture on your model.

Self-Evaluation Test

1. Briefly describe the texture palette.

2. Describe what the spotlight is all about and highlight 5 features of the spotlight.

3. Increase the intensity, hue, saturation, and contrast of a model.

4. Explain what poly painting is all about.

CHAPTER 10

UV MASTER

UVs are necessary for creating or utilizing a texture map in a 3D object. All three-dimensional programs use these two-dimensional coordinates to determine how to apply a texture to your object. Up until now, creating those UVs has been a labor-intensive process that requires a high degree of technical proficiency and leaves little opportunity for artistic expression.

The UV Master Plugin can create incredibly effective UVs for your models with only one click. You can easily and quickly create good UV maps that are ready to paint in a 2D painting program if you wish to work in 2D. UV Master's advanced technology allows you to delegate all technical tasks to the computer.

Introduction: UV Master

Unwrap All

Unwrap all perform the same procedure as Unwrap but on all accessible SubTools with full automated unwrapping. This action is ideal for unwrapping a large number of SubTools at once without the need to safeguard or attract the seams.

Symmetry

The UV unwrap will try to produce symmetrical results on the UV island when this option is selected. On some models, the plugin might trim the UV Island (s) to preserve symmetry. Note: While symmetry preservation is the plugin's top priority, it might not be possible on all models. It is impossible to achieve symmetrical unwrapping if the UV seam positions are not symmetric.

Polygroups

With the use of this option, you will design UV islands defined by currently existing poly groups of the model so that you can improve packing in the UV space. This is also another solution for you to further arrange your UV unwrap and minimize certain distortions.

The following is worth taking note of;

- The use of polygroups will accelerate the procedure.

- Please verify that your current polygroups are active before using this feature. By default, ZSpheres and ZSketch models generate polygroups automatically. However, an excessive number of polygroups might lead to an excessive number of UV islands, which can complicate the interpretation of the resulting UVs for texture development or future modification.

- Remember to make use of the many polygroup choices to rapidly and effectively create them with Polypainting or masking. Additionally, to ensure that there are no additional isolated polygroups, it is advised to make use of the **Tool > Visibility settings.**

Use Existing UV Seams

This capability is not limited to models that the plugin should unwrap without computing seams; it may also be used to load models that already have a UV or that have topology seams created by cutting the topology in another piece of software.

The plugin will use these topological seams or UV islands to create new UVs with a little stretching utilizing UV Master's advanced technique. Density Control painting can be used in this mode, but the Attract and Protect modes—which work solely on UV seams—will not be taken into account by the procedure.

The identical UV islands as in the originals will be present in the redesigned optimized UVs, but their borders will have a different shape. Put differently, the UV unwrapping on your model will be drastically different even if the actual cuts on it would be the same.

Note: UV Master will not be able to generate a UV unwrap without overlaps if the model has a specified topology, such as handles, or if it is only a closed volume without any topology cut or existing UV islands. When this option is enabled, the Symmetry and Polygroups choices are not available.

Enable Control Painting

UV Master Employs a Control Painting system to increase the quality of the UV unwrap, allowing you to submit additional information to the plugin, resulting in a more controlled output. To use this system, select **Enable Control Painting**. That will turn on the painting modes.

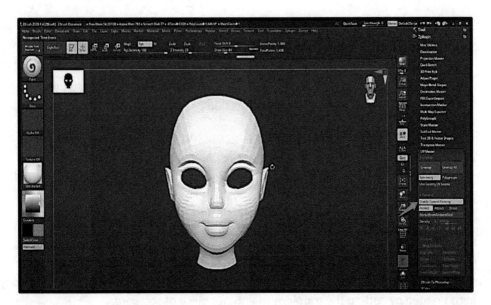

To make the Control Painting more visible, it is advised to use a white MatCap or the Work on Clone tool. The three operations that make up Control Painting are Protect, Attract, and Erase for UV Seam placement. In addition, there is a Density option that lets you adjust UV density to modify the pixel ratio between textures and UVs. The unwrap can simultaneously use any of these modes.

Protect

You can paint areas where you don't want seams to appear by utilizing this mode. To protect the component, the UV Master will use a value between 70% and 100% of the color value; a value considerably lower than this will not be used, which essentially implies that the UV seams creation will not be protected.

The unpainted area in the middle of a protection area, such as the interior of the mouth or nose, should receive extra attention when painting it. Although painting a loop around a neck would involve splitting the UVs into two islands, UV Master can fill in minor gaps. In this case, the plugin will require the creation of a seam even if the region is protected.

Attract

With this use of this mode, you can paint parts that will attract UV seams. Note that this is not a UV seams creation method and it also won't force the seams to part through it. This model is a very good addition to the protection one. This is the main reason why the two modes are usually visible in the same painting control map.

To alter the Attract color's strength, move the RGB intensity slider; a lower value indicates less seam attraction, and a higher value, greater seam attraction. It is advised to use 100% for this mode. The absence of paint does not mean that UV seams won't form in non-painted regions; UV Master will direct UV seams toward an Attract area but won't forbid them there.

Erase

With the use of this mode, you can erase the **Control Painting** that has been done with the Attract and Protect modes.

AttractFromAmbientOCCl

With the use of this tool, you can compute a dedicated Ambient Occlusion and change it to an Attract Control Paint. Just as there is a natural placing of the seams in less visible areas, it will also help with the improvement of the position of the UV seams where they happen to be less visible.

Density

With this mode, you can paint areas to change the pixel density by locally altering the UVs' scale. Using a high number means that your UV will occupy more space, which means it will use more pixels to create a more accurate texture. Reduced UV space usage results in a decreased resolution for that portion of the texture when the value is low. In addition, this mode comes in rather handy when you need to have more pixels on a character's face and less on their back or leg.

This Painting mode is combined with a Coefficient slider that affects the color of the painted areas, with settings ranging from 1 to 4, as well as an operator: multiply or divide.

First, choose the operator, then the value. 1 represents the UV size without modification, while 4 represents the UV size modulated by the multiply or divide operator.

Underneath the slider, there are preset buttons to expedite the process. You just need to press them to input the desired amount.

The picture uses a palette of hues that goes from green to white for positive values and cyan for negative values.

Use the ZBrush Smooth brushes to soften the Density color to create a more seamless transition between values. Recall to turn off Zadd and Zsub if required to avoid modifying the model's shape.

It is worthwhile if you would like to erase the parts of the density map, ensure you configure the density slider at 1 and paint over the painted parts.

Work On Clone

To ensure the UV works seamlessly to have a perfect understanding and also avoid any loss of data in the UV operation, the plugin will allow you to work with an already prepared copy of your model.

- When you click on the **Work on Clone utility of the plugin**, you will be able to clone the tool in use or SubTool and also get it ready for UV creation by going to the lowest level of subdivision, removing the higher levels, and modifying the current Matcap to the Skin4 Material.

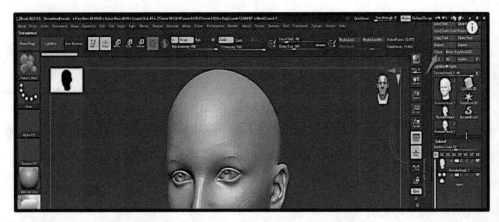

While not necessary, this step is highly advised because any poly painting that is currently in progress would be lost when utilizing more complex alternatives like Control Painting. Additionally, it stops the plugin from reprojecting details when it works with internal files—for example while utilizing the utilities called Unflatten and Flatten.

If all you want to do is click once to construct UVs on your model without changing or confirming the result, you don't need to work on a clone. For this reason, the default mode is not Work on Clone; rather, it is an option.

Copy UVs, Paste UVs

Once the unwrapping process on a clone model is finished, all you need to do is use the Copy UVS utility to copy the model UVs into memory, select the SubTool or basic Tool, and then use the Paste UVs utility to perform the transfer of the new UVs to this model through processing. Keep in mind that there is yet another way to transfer the UVs to several models with the same vertex order and topology.

Flatten, Unflatten

Since this flattened mesh is a 3D object, you can slightly change the UV representation with ZBrush brushes or tools. The Move or Smooth brushes will be used most frequently to locally modify or relax the UVs.

A common blunder is using the Smooth brush to relax the UVs. By doing this you will distort the UVs compared to the appropriate geometry, resulting in texture stretching.

UV Master Keeps as much of the relationship between the geometric shape and the generated UVs as possible.

- After finishing, click **UnFlatten** to return your flattened mesh to its 3D representation.

Check Seams

Upon selecting this mode, the model will display the UV seams as the poly painting is designed on it. The seams depiction will be updated whenever an action is taken that appears to impact the UV seams, such as unwrapping after making changes to the Control Painting.

The orange hue is used to highlight the UV seams, while the brown color is used to highlight the openings.

- This tool will operate with the seams generated by the plugin as well as any 3D model with UV seams. That is not the same as the UV Check feature featured in **ZBrush's Tool > Texture Map menu**.

Clear Maps

Information about Control Painting is stored by the UV Master in a special file called "Control Maps." During a ZBrush session, they are stored in the plugin's data folder and are associated with the Tool name.

This means that if you load a Tool with the same name as an earlier one that has had Control Painting applied to it, then activating Control Painting on the new one will result in the painting appearing on it. However, as the geometry of the two Tools may differ significantly, there may be several color anomalies.

Cleaning the Control Maps, as well as restarting ZBrush, will delete all temporary files.

LoadCtrlMap, and SaveCtrlMap

You can use the store or Load tools in the plugin's utility area to store or load your model's Control Painting in case you need to make changes to its UV unwrapping at a later time. Since their contents are erased upon each ZBrush restart, it is best to keep them with your ZTL files instead of in the UV Master data folder.

Self-Evaluation Test

1. Briefly describe UVmaster highlighting its features and applying them to a model.

CHAPTER 11

LIGHTING

Introduction: Light Palette

In addition to modifiers for additional flexibility, the Light palette has up to eight lights. You can turn on and off lights by clicking on them. A unified disk file can be created that contains the current lighting configuration—which includes all eight lights. In the same way, all eight lights can be changed by loading a file off the drive. Please note that adjustments made to the Light palette do not affect MatCap materials. Material for MatCaps has the light baked in.

Load and Save

The Load Lights button facilitates the definition of up to eight lights by loading a previously defined configuration. The loaded configuration has replaced and altered every light in this palette. Whether or not the eight lights are activated, the Save Lights button aids in saving them all, together with their responsive modifiers, to a single file.

Light Placement

You can change the position of the light using the **Light > Lights Placement sub-palette**. A Sun-type light's position is unaffected by the settings.

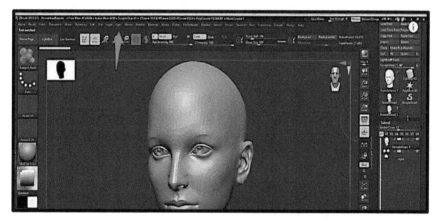

The Local Light Position Selector which usually is active just for point, spot, or glow lights can also be utilized in the choosing of the position of light on the canvas. Click on this button then move the canvas to choose the position at that point. The X, Y, and Z Position sliders will also be instantly updated.

XPos, YPos, and ZPos

The light's distance from the canvas's center can be adjusted using the Light Location sliders. These are set up automatically when you use the 'P' selection (above). Multiply these slider values by the average height and width of the page, then add the coordinates of the document's center to determine the coordinates of the light. These sliders are not functional when the light source is sunlight.

Radius

The Light Radius slider controls the falloff radius for point lights, the focal radius for spotlights, and the glow radius for glow lights. To convert this slider's value to pixols, multiply it by the document's average height and width.

Light Color

The selected light's color is displayed in the light color swatch. When the canvas is drawn using the Best Render mode, non-white colors will be visible. By picking this swatch just once, you can opt to change this color to the current color palette setting. To select the color at that precise location on the canvas or interface, you can also opt to click and drag this swatch.

Intensity

The slider of the light intensity helps with the determination of the brightness/dimness of the chosen light.

Ambient

The global ambient intensity slider not only controls the lighting effects produced by specific light sources but also sets the overall brightness of the document canvas. Materials can be defined independently of this light set by using their ambient intensities.

Distance

Global lights and environmental distance

Background

The **light > Background sub-palette** controls the setup and adjustments for a panoramic background.

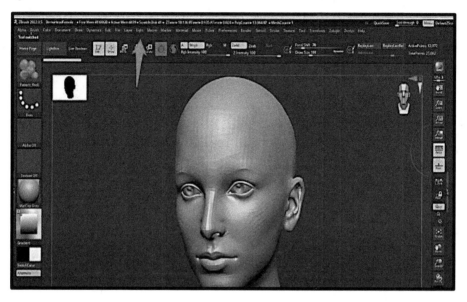

On

The ON button allows or restricts the display of the background image. This option is available only if a background image has been loaded.

Zoom

The Zoom slider enables you to zoom within the background image. It is simply possible for you to zoom in; you are unable to zoom out.

Create

This button helps with the creation of a new background with the use of the current document back color. The new background will then be displayed in the image thumbnail.

Image thumbnail

You can choose a background picture from the Texture palette when you click the Picture thumbnail. To find the necessary image, click the Import button located in the bottom left of the popup window if it hasn't been imported already.

Exposure

The Exposure slider allows you to adjust the image's exposure setting. This is helpful when dealing with 32-BIT pictures, such as HDRI, which have several exposure ranges.

Gamma

You can modify the loaded backdrop texture's gamma with the Gamma slider. You can darken shadows or highlight things that are hidden by shadows by doing this without changing the lighter regions of the image.

Longitude and Latitude

This slider enables you to rotate the background image on both the vertical and horizontal axes. This ensures that you can find the best point of view for the integration of your model with the image.

Tilt

The Tilt slider rotates the backdrop picture around the depth axis. When used with the Longitude and Latitude sliders, this feature enables you to rotate your backdrop in any direction across all axes.

Lightcap

To make a new Lightcap, utilize the LightCap sub-palette. Lightcap is a method of creating a Material or Matcap in real-time by controlling the lights they simulate directly.

Lightcap preview

You can adjust the light by dragging the dots that correspond to the LightCaps' locations in the preview window, which provides a real-time preview of the LightCaps. The Preview display can show the diffuse or specular information from the Lightcap.

The selected light is indicated by a red dot, and the unselected lights are represented by gray dots.

Since the default preview is displayed as a sphere instead of a 180° light positioning system, lights positioned on the sphere's side illuminate your model's back rather than its side. If you wish to illuminate the side, you will need to determine your light position.

NewLight

This button adds another light with its default configuration on the center of the Lightcap preview.

Del light

This button deletes the active light of the Lightcap preview.

Lightcap Adjustment

The LightCap Adjustment sub-palette has numerous functions that will modify or alter the current LightCap globally, as opposed to the LightCap settings, which only affect the selected light.

Exposure

This button enables you to add a multiplier on all light intensities of the Lightcap. This is very similar to the exposure in photography.

Hue

This slider enables you to modify the global hue of the Lightcap, which can allow you to modify its global color tint.

Saturation

The Saturation slider allows you to change the Lightcap's color. The color will lean more toward grayscale with a low saturation value, while the color saturation of the LightCap will be increased with a high number.

Intensity

You can adjust the color intensity altogether using the intensity slider. The entire Lightcap is affected equally by the linear effect; for an exponential effect, use Exposure.

Lightcap Horizon

The LightCap Horizon sub-palette has functions for altering the LightCap's orientation as well as generating and modifying a Horizon Line.

Horizon Opacity

The horizon line, which is made up of two gradients at the top and below the median line, is displayed by this slider. Its total ability is configured by the slider value.

Color C1 - C4

Make use of the C1 -C4 color selectors to specify the commencement and end colors of the bottom-to-top gradient of the horizon line.

Horizon Opacity O1 -O4

When you make use of the O1 - O4 sliders to modify the opacity of the corresponding C1 - C4 colors.

Rate Top and Rate Bottom

This slider configures the gradient change rate for both the top and bottom aspects of the horizon.

Lights Type

The buttons that can be found in the Light Type sub-palette determine the type of the chosen light.

Sun

Pressing the Sun Light button designates the light that is now selected as sunlight. Since there is no one place of origin for sunlight, all of its rays point in the same direction. The direction of the beams can be set using the Light Position window.

Point

The Point Light button changes the currently selected light to a point light, which casts light in all directions and emits light from a fixed point in space. The source point and falloff radius of a point light can be chosen using the modifiers in the Lights Placement menu.

Spot

By using this button, you can designate the selected light as a spotlight. Spotlights shine a light on a designated area of the canvas from a predetermined point in space. Using the modifiers in the lights placement menu, choose the spot radius and the source point. Use the light position window to change the direction that the spotlight faces.

Glow

The Glow Light button turns the currently selected light into a glowing light. Glow lights have a fixed glow radius and radiate from a specific place in space. Objects inside the glow radius are lighted evenly regardless of their orientation.

Using the modifiers in the Lights Placement menu, select the source point and the glow radius.

Radial

The Radial Light button changes the behavior of the chosen light type. Lights usually shine on objects that are right in front of them. When the Radial Light button is pressed, the chosen light illuminates surfaces that are turned away from it, which makes it a great 'fill' light for scenes. Radial lights do not cast shadows.

Lights Shadow

The sub-palette **Light > Lights Shadow** governs how the selected light casts shadows. Some of these options are only available for Best Renders. The Render palette is where BPR shadows are configured.

Intensity

The Shadow Intensity slider helps with the determination of the strength of the shadow cast by this light.

Shadow Curve

When rendering with Render: Best, Shadow Curve is applied. The shadow curve determines how shadows fade. For example, to create very black, hard-edged shadows, set the shadow curve to a straight line from the lower left to the top left, and then a straight line from the top left to the top right.

Length

The Shadow length slider determines the maximum length in pixols of the shadow cast by this light.

ZMode

ZBrush will estimate the shape of objects when producing this shadow when you click the ZMode Shadows button. 3D objects that are positioned on the ZBrush canvas and converted to pixols lose their surfaces that face away from the viewer. ZMode takes this into account while generating shadows, which usually produces better outcomes. If objects are not fully visible or are partially obscured, ZMode shadows might not be accurate.

Uni

The Unified Shadows slider brings down noise artifacts from standard ZMode shadows, giving rise to more unified shades and faster rendering. If the slider of the Ray is configured to a small value, this can lead to the production of more painterly shadows. This slider is active just when the ZMode button is tapped.

Blur

The Shadow Blur Radius slider shows how crisp or soft the edges of the shadows are. Much higher values give rise to softer shadows.

Rays

When calculating each pixol in this shadow, the Rays slider regulates the number of light rays that are included. Increased values lengthen the rendering time but produce more realistic shadows. Make the most of this slider when ZMode is enabled.

Aperture

The Aperture slider simulates a narrow or wide stream of light falling on objects, changing the sharpness of shadow edges. Sharper edges are produced by smaller numbers, which simulate a narrower light stream.

Environment Maps

The **Light > Environment sub-palette** regulates global environment illumination. The parameters are employed by any fresh LightCap that will automatically make the photos.

Gdm - Global Diffuse Map icon

To select the image used for diffuse shading in all light situations, select the Global Diffuse Map icon. Selecting images is done using the Texture palette pop-up; to import an image from the disk, select the Import button located on the bottom left of the pop-up. Complex light configurations can be replaced with Global Diffuse and Global Specular maps, freeing up the eight available lights for additional lighting effects.

Gsm - Global Specular Map icon

Choose the image in use for specular lighting in all light environments by clicking the Global Specular Map icon. Images are chosen from the Texture palette pop-up; to import an image from the disk,

- Click the **Import button** in the bottom left corner of the pop-up.

Global Diffuse and Global Specular maps can be used to replace complex light setups, freeing up the 8 available lights for other lighting effects.

Gdi - Global Diffuse Intensity

The Global Diffuse Intensity slider helps with the determination of the global diffuse shading defined by the Global Diffuse Map.

Gsi - Global Specular Intensity

The Global Specular Intensity slider helps with the determination of the strength of the global specular lighting specified by the Global Specular Map.

Self-Evaluation Test

1. Apply the modes in the light palette to a model. i.e. lightcap adjustment, lightcap horizon, light shadow.

CHAPTER 12

RENDERING

Introduction: KeyShot Renderer

ZBrush has various options for rendering both 2D and 3D work.

- By selecting **Document > Export**, you can export the finished render to a file. There are extra options for saving render passes for a BPR render that may subsequently be overlayed in an image editing tool.

Render Palette

Cursor

The Cursor button acts as a picker, allowing you to see a piece of the canvas in Best or Best Preview Render (BPR) mode. Click and drag this button to the canvas to use it.

Render

This button renders the whole image in the chosen render mode. Make use of this button after you have adjusted attributes that do not get updated instantly when they are modified.

Best

The best (and slowest) techniques are employed by the Best Renderer to produce the greatest quality image for the final render in 2D work. For 2D operations, shadows need to be rendered using this renderer.

ZBrush will switch to Preview Renderer mode if you attempt to work in Best Renderer mode. The Best Renderer will, however, merely re-render the object and its bounding box if you have a floating item in the scene and you change its material characteristics.

The Best Renderer button causes the canvas to be rendered in Best Render mode. Shadows, reflections, antialiasing, global illumination, and other advanced features are added by Best Renderer. Each effect must first be activated using the palette's adjustment icons and modifiers.

- Use the **ESC key** to cancel rendering and revert to Preview Render mode.

Preview

The renderer that is utilized by default is employed when creating a scene or sculpting. Most of the scene's elements, such as Preview Shadows, will be visible, but some material and other effects, like fog, light hues, depth cues, and shadows from the light palette won't be. It does show transparency, but for the most part, it is not as good as the Best renderer.

The canvas is rendered when the Preview Renderer button is in the Preview Render mode. Preview Render, the default render mode, displays traditional lighting and material effects. Real-time representations are available for most painting and sculpting properties.

Fast

The canvas renders in Fast Render mode when the Fast Renderer button is pressed. In Quick Render mode, nothing is rendered with much shading and all material attributes are disregarded. When sculpting complex objects, you might occasionally want to use Fast Render mode because it minimizes editing reaction time.

Flat

This option enables you to view the scene with no shading, just basic shading. This makes it quite ideal for modeling since it is quite fast and displays surface details due to geometry, not materials.

External Renderer

KeyShot

This enables the bridge between ZBrush and KeyShot. When this option is enabled, anytime you ask ZBrush to perform a BPR render it will instantly send your model to KeyShot. If this option is disabled, ZBrush will make use of its own BPR renderer.

Max Faces

The existing model is divided into smaller parts by the Max Faces model. Each potion's size will not exceed the predetermined limits set by this slider. Your work will be sent to KeyShot in larger portions as you increase the slider's value. Depending on how your computer is set up, this could cause lags or even cause the Bridge to hang entirely.

Think about going over a footbridge. If you attempted to drive a tank across, it would probably collapse. However, you may reassemble the tank on the other side if you dismantle it and carry it across in bits. The specs of your system dictate the actual capacity of your bridge. Keeping the value low will lead to smaller pieces of data being sent to KeyShot, which will usually speed up the process—even if your machine is powerful.

If the Auto Merge option is enabled, KeyShot will combine these smaller portions.

Auto Merge Mode

ZBrush can send enormous amounts of data to KeyShot, therefore to expedite the Bridge process, the data must typically be divided into smaller parts. The Auto Merge mode will then instruct KeyShot to join all of these components to reconstruct the models exactly as they were in ZBrush.

Naturally, increasing the Max Faces Slider value will allow data to be transferred in bigger chunks, avoiding model splitting. However, since there is a 10 million polygon limit, you will almost definitely need to combine certain elements of your model at some point.

If you don't have an Auto Merge set, your KeyShot scene can have a lot of components. Therefore, turning on Auto Merge is highly recommended.

So, why would you ever want to disable Auto Merge? You may wish to do fast renderings of your models while working and will not be adding KeyShot-specific materials through the Scene tree. In that instance, turning off Auto Merge will speed up the Bridge operation because KeyShot won't have to spend time welding the model back together.

Group by Materials

This mode facilitates the process of creating a distinct group for every ZBrush material that is added to the sub-tools' models. This essentially indicates that KeyShot will generate an equal number of material groups for each type of material you add to your model in ZBrush.

These groups are defined by the materials in ZBrush; no further visual aid is available. Once the model is submitted to KeyShot, you can apply materials from the KeyShot library to any section of the model that belongs to a material group by dragging those materials onto the relevant piece of the model.

When this option is deactivated, each model is independent, and dragging material from the KeyShot library onto the model affects only that model.

Send Document Color

The Transmit Document Color mode instructs KeyShot to adjust its document backdrop color to match your ZBrush document when activated.

This function doesn't send any background image to KeyShot; it merely sends the color values obtained in the Document palette.

Render Properties

Preview Render Maps Detail Level. By using the Details slider, you can improve the render's aesthetic attractiveness. To do this, bigger maps will be created for the **Light > Environment Maps**. This will also affect how well Lightcap is produced from a background image. These environment maps govern the overall quality of material creation.

If you're looking for quick renderings or Lightcap creation, leave it at 1. Once your settings are perfect, you can generate environment maps with a higher dynamic range by raising the Details slider, which will produce the best possible final render.

The Diffuse and Specular maps generated by the LightCap process are 512512 pixels when the Details slider is set to 1 and increase to 20482048 pixels when set to 3.

3D Posterize

This slider adds posterization to a 3D model notwithstanding the materials that have been added to it. This renders 3D posterization works by modifying the normals for the entire model such that the light falling on the model is split into blocks and the colors are flattened. It offers a very fast way of generating a posterized render though without the light control that modifying materials offers.

Smooth Normals

Enabled is the BPR Smooth Normals Render Mode. With BPR in this mode, you won't need to add more subdivision levels to get a smoother surface. With this rendering setting, BPR is instructed to instantaneously smooth the edges between polygons, producing a perfectly smooth model surface.

To use this mode, you should also enable the **Tool > Display Properties >Smooth Normal option for any Tool or SubTool(s)** that you want the BPR to smooth. This implies you can change the render smoothness for individual surfaces as needed.

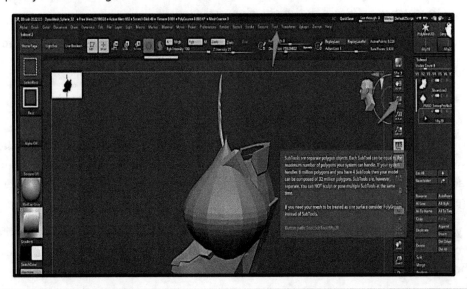

Materials Blend - Radius

the distance at which nearby elements combine. By increasing the Blend Radius parameter, ZBrush will blend the areas on a model's surface where materials intersect. This removes abrupt changes between materials that have radically differing properties.

A mix with a very brief/narrow changeover and a very strong effect is produced by a low value. A high value produces a very soft look and a broad transition for blending.

This Material blending value has a global effect on the entire model. If you want to manipulate particular SubTools, you must additionally modify the BPR Material Blender slider in that object's **Tool > Display Properties menu**.

BPR Render Pass

By employing the BPR renderer, different passes are instantly accessible. You may find them in the **Render > BPR RenderPass sub-palette**.

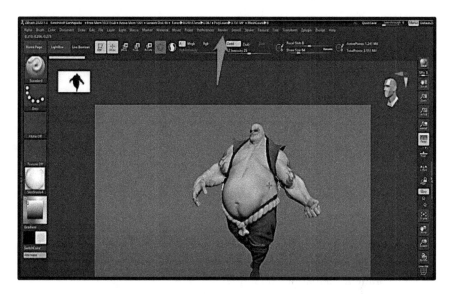

- To save a certain pass, click **on its symbo**l.

After that, a Save As window will appear, giving you the option to save the file to disk in one of several image formats. Before executing the render, you must enable the option for some passes, such as Shadow and Ambient Occlusion, in the Render > Render Properties sub-palette. Since these parameters were not enabled, AmOc (ambient occlusion) and Sss (sub-surface scattering) are not available in the example above.

BPR Transparency

Strength

The Transparency effect by surface normals is controlled by the Strength slider. A greater value will provide more openness.

NFactor

This slider controls the Transparency affected by surface normals. It controls the falloff between transparent and opaque portions of the mesh as a result of the normal direction. A configuration of 0 means that all aspects of the mesh will be visible and a configuration of 1 means that just normals that face the viewer directly will be visible.

ByColor

This slider controls the Transparency effect via color intensity. A higher value will offer much greater transparency.

CFactor

The CFactor slider is used to adjust the color intensity factor: Better color separation is achieved with larger values. Set to 1, the mesh is completely transparent, while set to 0 there is no difference in color. The most variation is achieved with a setting of 4, where white areas are fully opaque and black sections are fully transparent.

Refract

The slider controls the quantity of refraction; higher values offer more exaggerated refraction, effectively multiplying the configuration of the Refract slider. Configuration to a much higher value for a magnifying lens effect.

BPR Shadow

The BPR Shadow sub-palette controls just how the shadows are rendered with the Best Preview Render.

FStrength

This slider configures the strength for shadows cast on the floor; much higher values offer a stronger shadow, for shadows to display on the floor; the Floor Grid must be activated.

GStrength

You don't need to adjust the **Material > Environment >Shadow slider settings** for each material separately to adjust the amount of shadow applied to your entire model thanks to the Global Shadow Strength slider. A stronger shadow is produced with a higher value.

Keep in mind that you can adjust this slider independently for different materials to fine-tune the shadows as needed. This slider is an exponent of all **Material > Environment > Shadow slider settings**. For instance, if you set the Environment Shadow of one of your materials to 100 and then lower the Global Shadow Strength to 50, the material will only receive half of the 100 value.

Rays

This slider will configure the number of rays utilized in the calculation of the shadow. A greater number will offer softer shadows based on the Angle settings. Increasing the ray number will boost render time.

Angle

The Angle slider determines the greatest angle at which the rays can be generated: Higher values produce softer, less defined shadows. A 360 setting with a large number of rays will produce an effect similar to ambient occlusion.

Res

The shadows' pixel resolution is set with the Res slider: This picture shows the image size (independent of document size) that ZBrush internally uses for shadow calculations. Higher settings offer more accuracy, but lower settings render more quickly. For example, if soft shadows are needed, a lower number can achieve the desired effect with less processing overhead.

Blur

This slider will configure shadow blur radius in pixels: greater values offer softer, more blurred shadows. This is concerning the Res slider and ought to be modified in tandem for the same effect.

VDepth

The view depth offset, or how far the shadow computation is offset from the spectator (with positive values) or toward them (with negative values), is controlled by the VDepth slider. Positive values increase the total shade, whereas negative numbers intensify the light and shadows.

LDepth

To lighten the depth offset in pixels, use the LDepth slider: The shadow computation is shifted in the direction of the light source (positive values) or away from it (negative values). Positive values produce more overall darkness, while negative values might intensify the light and shadows.

Max Dist

This slider controls just how far shadows sketch. A much higher value offers longer shadows with a configuration of 10 offering the longest shadows. The default configuration of 0 disables this option- shadows will be at their longest.

Bpr Ao

Strength

Ambient Occlusion Strength. The strength slider configures the strength of the ambient occlusion effect; a much higher value offers a stronger effect.

Color

The color button configures the color of the ambient occlusion; color is not added to the AO map designed when the Create Maps option is turned on.

Angle

The Angle slider ought to be left at 360 but reducing the value will slim the AO effect concerning light direction.

Res

The ambient occlusion (AO) resolution in pixels can be adjusted using the Res slider. This is the image size (not the document size) that ZBrush internally uses to calculate ambient occlusion. Higher settings offer more accuracy, but lower settings render more quickly. For example, if a faint AO effect is needed, a lower number can provide the desired outcome with less processing overhead.

Gamma

The gamma of ambient occlusion is adjusted by the gamma slider; gamma and AO effect brightness are the same. Overall ambient occlusion gets darker at lower values and lighter overall ambient occlusion at higher values. A setting of five should work well in the majority of situations.

Bpr Sss

SSS Acros Subtools

SSS is calculated over all sub-tools. While computing subsurface scattering, the SSS across Subtools button takes into account all sub-tools. When this button is deactivated, SSS is calculated as if each sub-tool were lighted independently.

Res

The Res slider determines the resolution of the SSS in pixels: This is the image size (unrelated to document size) that ZBrush uses internally to calculate subsurface scattering. Lower settings render faster, but higher settings provide greater accuracy. When a faint SSS effect is required, for example, a lower value can provide the intended effect with less processing overhead.

Blur

The SSS blur radius is adjusted in pixels using the Blur slider; softer, blurrier subsurface scattering is produced by larger values. This should be adjusted in conjunction with the Res slider to achieve the desired result. For instance, the Blur value should increase from 4 to 8 if the Res slider value is raised from 500 to 1000.

BPR Filter

BPR filters are post-processing effects that you can apply to your Best Preview Render. There are various advantages to employing these filters. For starters, it eliminates the need to perform post-rendering work in software such as Photoshop. Second, BPR filters can make use of internally computed information such as depth or masking. This implies you can add the effects to a specific section of the image rather than the entire image. This local application of the filters is also what distinguishes BPR filters from prior versions of ZBrush render filters.

F1- F8

To view the matching slot that can receive a filter, use the F1 through F8 buttons. There aren't any filters active by default. To enable or disable the filter, you must click the small circle located in the upper right corner of the Function button.

Filter (default > Noise)

The Filter picker. Click to choose a filter for your render. The same filter can be used in many slots, each with its own set of settings.

BlendMode (default > Add)

Set the mode whereby the filter effect is applied to your render. Each filter has a default blend mode that is selected by default, but you can adjust it to achieve the exact result you want.

Strength

Select the level of filtration strength that will be used on your render. At zero, the filter has no effect; at one, it has a 100% effect. It is also possible to use negative values, which will have the opposite effect on the filter (e.g., converting the Blur filter to a Sharpen filter).

Mask

Modification of Mask Strength. The model's profile affects the filter. The filter will only be applied to the areas of the canvas that your model covers when it is set to its highest value. The filter only affects the backdrop when set to -1. It is not necessary to activate this data in the render options to add it to the image; it is always available.

Shadow

Shadow can be used to adjust strength. Controls which sections of the surface are in shadow by modifying the filter. At its peak value, the filter will only be employed where there are shadows in the render. This data is always accessible and does not need to be activated in the Render settings before it can be applied to the image.

AO

AO allows for the adjustment of strength. Depending on how near the surfaces are to one another, the filter is altered. The filter will only be applied in render zones where Ambient Occlusion shadows are cast when it is set to its highest value. Only if you enable ambient occlusion in the **Render > Render Properties sub-palette** before rendering will this information be visible.

SSS

SSS is used to modify strength. Modifies the filter's SSS parameters to control where light can travel through the model. When set to its maximum value, the filter will only be applied to the render's translucent portions.

- Only when Sub Surface Scattering is enabled in the **Render >Render Properties sub-palette** before rendering is this information available.

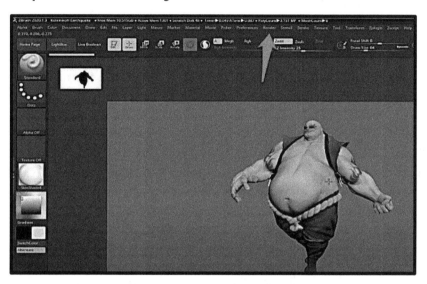

Int

Filter By Color Intensity. The intensity of the color picked in the related Color Swatch is used to modify a filter. The size of the intensity roll-off applied to the model is controlled by the Int Exp slider. Higher values will cause the filter to affect less of the render.

Hue

Hue Color Filter. A filter can be altered by changing the hue of the color selected in the corresponding Color Swatch. The hue roll-off that is applied to the model's hue is set via the Hue Exp slider. The filter will have less of an impact on the render at higher settings.

Sat

Color Saturation Filter. The saturation of the color picked in the related Color Swatch is used to modify a filter. The Sat Exp slider controls the amount of saturation roll-off given to the model. Higher values will cause the filter to affect less of the render.

Antialiasing

Blur

The color antialiasing slider is utilized only by the Best Renderer and helps with the determination of the softness of the anti-aliasing effect. Bigger values show more blurring. Antialiasing is an edge-blurring effect that ensures that rendered images show smoother even when their pixol resolutions are low.

Edge

The Edge Antialiasing slider is only available to the Best Renderer and defines how harsh an edge or corner must be before antialiasing is applied. When this number is set to 0, only sharp edges are antialiased; when set to 100, all edges are antialiased.

SuperSample

The Super Sample slider is only used by the Best Renderer. To achieve the optimal antialiasing effect, ZBrush can compute antialiasing parameters for the full image several times and average the results. This slider, with values ranging from 1 (the default) to 4, determines how many times the entire image is calculated. While rendering times are greatly increased, higher settings produce better results.

Depth Cue

Depth cues lead the image to be produced with varying degrees of blur at various depths. This can be used to replicate the effect of a lens that only focuses sharply at one depth or atmospheric haze, which makes distant objects appear blurrier.

- **Depth Cue Alpha:** You can adjust the depth cue effect with Depth Cue Alpha. Click the Depth Cue Alpha patch to open the texture sub-palette, then choose a texture. It will be converted to grayscale alpha and stretched across the entire canvas area. Each alpha pixol at that place controls the depth cue's intensity. The influence of depth cues is greatest in white areas and absent in black ones. This helps to focus the depth cue effect on a particular region of the painting.

- **Depth 1**: Depth1 is the near point of the depth cue effect. There's no blurring at this range. The blurring starts when depth increases. To set the value, either directly type in the Z depth or click and drag an object from the slider to the canvas; after

151

selecting an object at the depth at which you want the depth cue to begin, release the mouse button.

- **Depth 2**: this is the far portion of the depth cue effect. There is total blurring at this distance. Type in the Z depth straightaway or click and drag from the slider to the canvas to choose a depth.

Fog

When utilizing Best Render, the Fog subpalette gives settings for obtaining a fog effect; different depths or regions of the canvas may be partially or completely veiled by a foggy or smoky haze.

- **Depth 1:** Depth1 is the fog effect's closest point. At this distance, there is no fog effect. As depth grows, so does the fog effect. To set the value, type in the Z depth immediately or click and drag from the slider to the canvas; select an object a pixol at the level you want the fog to begin.

- **Depth 2**: this is the very far point of the effect of the fog. There is a full fog at this distance. Configure the value as for Depth1.

- **Fog Color 1**: Fog Color 1 is the color of the fog around the fog effect's center. Set by choosing a color from the color pickers and clicking on the Fog Color 1 patch. You can also select a color by dragging it from Fog Color 1 to any region of the canvas or interface.

- **Fog Texture**: A bitmap texture can also be used to colorize the fog. With a fog texture, you may create different environmental effects such as smog. To access the texture sub-palette and select a texture,

  - **Click and hold on to the Fog Texture patch**.

It will be extended across the full canvas. Each texture pixel determines the hue of the fog at that point.

- **Fog Alpha:** Fog Alpha can be used to further customize the fog effect. To view the texture sub-palette and select a texture,

  - **Click and hold on to the Fog Alpha patch**.

152

It will be spread across the full canvas area as a grayscale alpha. The strength of the fog at that position is determined by each alpha pixel. There is the most fog when the alpha is white. There is no fog effect when the alpha is black.

Preview Shadows

ObjShadow

This controls the intensity of the real-time shadow of the model.

DeepShadow

The preview shadows will get more intense when you press this button. The shadows will have a wider gradient range from surface interesting places when this is enabled.

Length

Extend the scan range used by ZBrush to generate the shadow. A longer length lengthens and softens the shadow but increases computation time.

Slope

Describes the light's angle at which the shadow was produced. Every shadow on the canvas falls at a 45-degree angle. It is impossible to alter this. A slope determines the angle in Y at which the light casts shadows. When the value is zero, the model's overhead light is the source of light. The light is closer to the model when the number is higher.

Depth

This option deepens and also enlarges the shadow. The effect of the depth is based on the configuration for the slope; at the very little configuration of the slope, modifying Depth will have very little effect.

Preview Wax

Using the Preview render, Preview Wax will give the model's materials a waxy look in real-time.

This suggests that the effect will be felt even when the scene is being normally sculpted and set up.

Make sure the Strength slider in the **Material > Wax Modifiers menu** is set above zero and activate the WaxPreview option in the **Render > Render Properties menu** to see Preview Wax.

Strength

The Strength slider controls how much wax effect is applied to the model. A high value will cause the model to seem waxy, while a low value will produce a mild SSS-like effect.

Fresnel

The slider indicates whether the wax effect should be applied to the model's face-facing surface or its tilted off-camera surfaces. The surface's sides will be impacted by a positive value, while the front of the surface will be affected by a negative value.

Radius

The radius slider determines how far the wax effect stretches out from the areas determined by your other parameters to be waxy. A low number reduces the area of the wax, whilst a high value increases the amount of wax rendered throughout the model's surface.

Temperature

The Temperature slider influences the wax temperature, much to the light temperature in photography. A negative number tints the wax cold (blue), while a positive value tints it hot (red).

Environment

The **Render > Environment subpalette**

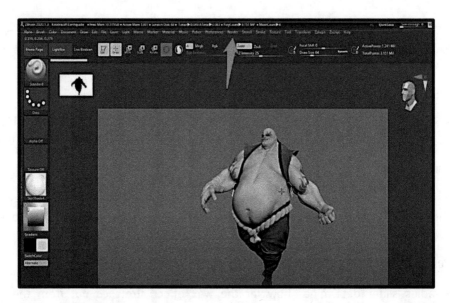

Allows you to globally reflect one image or color onto all of the scene's reflective surfaces. Each material's ambient reflection amount is controlled within the Material palette. You can only use the best renderer to get this effect.

Controls

Off: This turns off Color, Texture, or Scene reflections.

Colors: When this is turned on, it enables you to make use of just one color for global reflections. When you press the color button, it enables the Environment Color Patch.

Txtr: this enables a texture to be utilized for global reflections. Pressing the Texture button allows the Environment Texture patch.

Scene: When this is turned on, it makes use of the current scene as a source image for global reflections.

Environment

Use this patch to alter the environment's color whenever the Color switch is used. Select a color using any of the color pickers, then click Environment Color. Alternatively, you can click and drag **Environment Color** to choose a color from almost any area of the canvas or interface.

Adjustments

Color changes to the final render can be made using the **Render > Adjustments settings** without permanently affecting it. The four curves at the bottom of this subpalette are the RGB Level, Red Level, Green Level, and Blue Level adjustment curves, in that order. To open a curve, click on it.

Controls

Adjust: Adjustment variables are enabled. After the values have been altered, the Adjust button can be used to toggle the adjustments on and off. The ZBrush scene file contains all adjustment values.

ZPlugin Palette

Brush

Helps with the reduction of the current Draw size by the amount in the slider of the brush increment.

Brush Increment

The Brush Increment slider controls how much the Draw Size increases/decreases when you use the **Brush & Brush> buttons or hotkeys**.

Homepage

The Home Page button will open the Home Page where you can read about the latest ZBrushCore or Pixologic news, gain access to various tutorials, and a lot more.

Decimation Master

A simplified version of Decimation Master is provided to enable model optimization for 3D printing. To automatically reduce the number of polygons in your model, just choose one of the five preset buttons. You can alter the setting without having to undo everything if you find that too much data has been lost.

Self-Evaluation Test

1. Mention five features in the render palette.

2. Menton 3 features of the ZPlugin palette.

CHAPTER 13

DYNAMICS

Introduction to Dynamics

The Dynamic Subdivision system provides alternatives to ZBrush's Traditional Subdivision Surface mode, permitting you to add dynamic smoothing to your models without really separating the polygons. This function is primarily intended to operate in conjunction with the ZModeler brush and low polygonal models.

Dynamics Palette

Simulation Iterations

This aids in managing the number of simulation cycles that are needed for every movement. Although larger values result in more precision, they may slow down the simulation. Because the simulation does not have enough time to adjust to the form change, smaller values will result in more stretching. 50 is the default value.

Strength

The cloth strength slider affects just how much the surface area is kept together. Lower values might mean the cloth will tend to have more stretch.

Firmness

This slider affects the way the surface will tend to wrinkle and fold. Lower values will offer more folds and wrinkles. This slider can also be used to simulate various weights or types of fabric.

On Masked

You can navigate the unmasked region by applying the simulation to the masked portion. This makes it possible to create unique structures like, say, carpet rolls. The masked portions of the model will be ignored by the simulation and fabric brushes if this is left unchecked.

On Brushed

With this option, the brush's single portion will have simulation added to it. It enables the effect to be used on a geometry with significantly more polygons. Use the Fade Border slider to control the amount of fading.

Turn off On Brushed in order to have the simulation affect the entire mesh.

Fade Border

This option fades the simulation effect when the ON Brushed is being employed. A much higher value will provide more fading. A configuration of 0 turns off fading.

Self-Collision

When the object collides with itself, it will react to avoid overlapping geometry. A higher value will result in better detection of self-collision. The maximum setting is 4, and a value of 0 indicates that self-collision is disabled.

Floor Collision

In this option, the simulation will react to the floor grid within ZBrush. Turn off to take off floor collision. The floor height can be modified in the Draw palette with the Elv slider.

Allow Shrink

This button will cause the surface to shrink to the same size as all surfaces underneath it. Surface stretching may result from this. Folds and creases will appear if a morph target has been saved since it will expand back to its original size when turned off and then touched.

Allow Expand

By using this option, it is possible to enlarge the mesh area as much as using the Cloth Pull brush. Turning off the option and touching the mesh will cause it to contract back to its original size if a morph target has been saved and the mesh expansion causes stretching.

Gravity

Gravity is applied uniformly to all regions of the mesh. Working with a low-resolution mesh and **Tool > Geometry > Dynamic Subdiv > Thickness allows a thin**, variable-thickness surface to interact with gravity.

Liquify

This modifies the dynamics algorithm from cloth liquid.

Set Direction

By default, gravity is programmed to move from the top to the bottom of the ZBrush window. The direction of the model can be altered by you. Simply turn your model so that the ZBrush canvas's necessary direction runs from top to bottom.

- To save that angle, click **Set Direction**. Gravity will then be applied in the desired way relative to the model, regardless of how the model is rotated on the canvas.

Gravity Strength

The force of gravity was used. Larger numbers will result in a faster simulation, which may result in more mesh stretching based on the Simulation Iterations setting.

Inflate, Inflate Amount

The mesh area will be stretched by the simulation. Face-facing polygons are pushed outward in that direction. The simulation's speed can be adjusted using the Inflate Amount slider. To halt the simulation on any axis, use the XYZ buttons. For instance, deactivate X and Y to simply cause inflation along the Z axis. The Z will stay white, while the X and Y will turn gray.

The Inflate amount is the rate at which the mesh will expand when the Inflate option is activated.

Deflate, Deflate Amount

The simulation will result in a smaller mesh region. Polygons are rotated from their present orientation in reverse. The Deflate Amount slider sets the simulation speed.

The simulation is restricted to any axis by the XYZ buttons. Deactivate X and Y, for instance, if you just want the Z axis to deflate. The Z will stay white while the X and Y become grayscale. The Deflate amount is the rate at which the mesh will expand when the Deflate option is activated.

Expand, Expand Amount

Expand helps with the growth of the surface area, rippling it. Points are usually moved away from each other in all directions. The speed at which the mesh will grow when the Expand option is switched on is known as the Expand Amount.

Contract, Contract Amount

The simulation will result in a smaller mesh region. Points are shifted toward one another in all directions. The simulation speed is adjusted via the Contract Amount slider. The mesh shrinkage rate, when the Contract option is on, is referred to as the Contract Amount.

Collision Volume

Compute the Collision Volume. If this switch is not active the simulation will then not react to anything in your scene.

Recalc

Once your scenario has been modified, click the Recalc button. This covers moving or adding SubTools in addition to turning on or off the SubTool display. The simulation will continue to function as if a SubTool is still present even if it is turned off or deleted without first pressing Recalc.

Resolution

This option controls the smoothness of the collision volume. A low value like 128, will offer a very "blocky" result. Note that values that are higher are the very best.

Inflate

The Collision Volume Inflate slider determines how much the collision volume is "inflated," causing the cloth to react slightly above the surface. Reduce this slider for tighter clothes.

Run Simulation

The fabric simulation is started. To pause the simulation, click any area of the document backdrop or press the Spacebar. Then, before hitting the button again to resume the simulation, mask any parts you want to maintain as they are.

Max Simulation Points

The maximum point value above which the simulation is not available. A mesh of 250,000 points is produced by the default setting of 250 because the slider value is in the 1000s. Any attempt to simulate cloth on a mesh that has a density higher than this will not work. This slider raises the threshold; nevertheless, you might not see the desired outcomes until you adjust the Gravity Strength and Simulation Iterations parameters as well. Low polygon meshes are well suited for using cloth simulations. Once you've gotten the desired effect, you may apply the subdivisions after using Dynamic Subdiv to provide a high-resolution preview.

Self-Evaluation Test

1. Describe 5 features of the dynamic palette.

CONCLUSION

ZBrush is a digital sculpting and coloring program whose potent features and simple workflows have revolutionized the 3D industry. ZBrush, with its visually appealing interface, offers the most potent tools available to modern digital artists. ZBrush provides a user experience that feels incredibly natural and inspires the artist within with an arsenal of tools designed with simplicity in mind. ZBrush's ability to sculpt up to one billion polygons means that the only limitations on your creations are your imagination.

Based on the premise of circularity, the menus in ZBrush interact together in a non-linear and mode-free method.

With ZBrush, you have access to all the tools you need to quickly draw up a 2D or 3D design and see it through to completion. With ZBrush, you can create precise renderings with lighting and ambient effects right away. You may easily prepare your model for 3D printing or use it in any other digital application by selecting one of the many robust export options.

ZBrush's powerful software processing allows users to sculpt and paint with millions of polygons without the need to purchase costly graphics cards. Because of this, ZBrush is used by everyone from large film and game firms to amateur artists.

Leave technical difficulties and steep learning curves behind, as you sculpt and paint with recognizable brushes and tools.

INDEX

3

3D Posterize, **152**

A

All High, **71**, **79**
All Low, **71**, **79**
Allow Shrink, **6**, **168**
Alpha 3D Vector, **41**
Alphas, **52**, **104**, **110**, **111**, **122**
Alt + Shift pressed, **122**, **123**
Alt Pressed, **123**
Ambient, **114**, **135**, **140**, **153**, **156**, **159**
Antialiasing, **160**
AO, **156**, **157**, **159**
Aperture, **146**
Append, **65**, **72**, **79**, **81**, **89**
Append New, **65**
Array Mesh, **61**, **62**, **64**, **66**
Array Meshes, **66**
ArrayMesh, **62**, **63**, **64**, **65**, **67**, **68**, **75**
arrow, **4**, **19**, **69**, **70**, **111**
Arrow Buttons, **69**
AutoReorder, **71**

B

Back, **103**, **122**
BevelPro, **76**
Blob, **43**
Blur, **57**, **95**, **146**, **155**, **157**, **158**, **160**
Boolean, **75**, **76**, **93**, **95**, **119**, **122**, **123**
BPR Filter, **157**
BPR Render Pass, **153**
BPR Shadow, **154**
Bridge Constraints, **38**
Brush, **23**, **24**, **25**, **26**, **28**, **29**, **31**, **32**, **34**, **35**, **36**, **40**, **44**, **79**, **110**, **111**, **165**
Bulge, **41**
ByColor, **154**

C

Canvas Document, **18**
CFactor, **154**
Chain, **66**

Clay, **44**, **86**
Clip Brushes, **28**, **29**
Clone, **53**, **104**, **118**, **125**, **126**, **131**, **134**, **136**
Collision, **170**
Color, **40**, **59**, **82**, **116**, **118**, **129**, **140**, **144**, **151**, **156**, **159**, **160**, **162**, **164**, **165**
Colors, **59**, **164**
Colors Option, **59**
Contract, **170**
Contrast, **126**, **127**
Control Painting, **133**, **134**, **135**, **136**, **137**, **138**
Controls, **59**, **158**, **164**, **165**
Copy, **53**, **58**, **66**, **137**
Copy Tool, **53**
CopyMat, **5**, **112**
CopySH, **114**
CropAndFill, **119**
Cursor, **148**
Curve, **29**, **30**, **36**, **37**, **39**, **103**, **145**
Curve Brushes, **29**

D

Deflate, **169**, **170**
Deformation Option, **60**
Del light, **143**
Del Lower, **55**, **99**
Del Other, **73**
Delete, **37**, **66**, **72**, **79**, **122**
Density, **25**, **55**, **82**, **92**, **97**, **98**, **133**, **134**, **135**, **136**
Depth, **31**, **32**, **118**, **161**, **163**
Depth Cue, **161**
Diffuse, **115**, **146**, **147**, **151**
Digital Sculpting, **4**, **46**, **47**, **52**
Displace, **43**
Duplicate, **62**, **71**, **79**, **122**
Dynamesh, **94**, **98**, **99**, **100**
DynaMesh, **4**, **29**, **35**, **45**, **92**, **93**, **94**, **95**, **96**, **99**, **100**
Dynamic Symmetry, **3**
Dynamics, **6**, **167**

E

Edge, **160**
Elastic, **43**
Env. Reflection, **116**
Environment, **146**, **151**, **155**, **164**, **165**
Environment Maps, **146**, **151**

Expand, 6, **123**, **168**, **170**
Exponent, **113**
Export, **5**, **53**, **110**, **118**, **148**
Exposure, **142**, **143**
External Renderer, **149**
Extract, **78**
Extrude, **67**

F

Fade, 60, **120**, **121**, **168**
Fade Option, **60**
FiberMesh, 4, **32**, **78**, **79**, **80**
Fil H- Mirror H, **123**
FillLayer, **118**
Firmness, **167**
Flatten, **44**, **136**, **137**
Flip V - Mirror V, **124**
Floor Collision, **168**
Flush, **40**, **41**
FlushDynamic, **40**
FlushResize, **40**
Frame, **36**, **123**
FreezeGroup, **97**
Fresnel, **113**, **163**
Front, **122**
FStrength, **154**

G

Gamma, **142**, **157**
Geometry, **37**, **49**, **55**, **56**, **83**, **99**, **101**, **107**, **169**
Glow, **145**
GrabDoc, **5**, **52**, **119**
Groom, 4, **32**, **33**, **34**, **78**
Groom Brushes, **32**
Groomer Magnet, **33**
Groomer Strong, **33**
Groomer Twist, **33**
Groups, **25**, **27**, **74**, **94**, **97**
Groups Split, **74**
GStrength, **155**

H

Hide/Restore/Close, **18**
Higher Res, **55**
Hot Keys, **22**
Hue, **128**, **143**, **160**

I

Image thumbnail, **141**
Import, **5**, **17**, **53**, **118**, **141**, **146**, **147**
Inflat, **42**
Inflate, **42**, **43**, **169**, **170**
Insert, **29**, **35**, **63**, **65**, **72**, **79**, **96**
Insert New, **65**
Int, **159**, **160**
Intensity, **26**, **36**, **43**, **45**, **82**, **120**, **126**, **127**, **128**, **129**, **140**, **143**, **145**, **147**, **159**

K

KeyShot Renderer, 6, **148**

L

Layer, **45**, **118**
LDepth, **156**
Length, **145**, **162**
Light Palette, **139**
Light Placement, **139**
Lightbox, **18**, **31**, **104**, **110**, **111**, **112**
Lightcap, **142**, **143**, **144**, **151**
Lighting, 5, 6
Lights Shadow, **145**
Lights Type, **144**
List All, **69**
Lock, **64**
Longitude and Latitude, **142**
Lower Res, **55**

M

Macintosh, **7**, **8**
Magnify, **43**, **45**
MakeAlpha, **118**
Mask, **2**, **57**, **102**, **103**, **105**, **158**
Mask Region, **2**
Masking, **56**, **105**
Material, **19**, **23**, **59**, **109**, **110**, **111**, **112**, **114**, **116**, **136**, **139**, **142**, **153**, **155**, **163**, **164**
Material Option, **59**
Materials, **5**, **19**, **59**, **109**, **110**, **112**, **116**, **140**, **151**, **152**
Max Dist, **156**
Max Faces, **150**
Max Simulation Points, **171**
Merge, **75**, **79**, **99**, **150**
MergeDown, **75**
MergeSimilar, **75**
Metallicity, **115**

Modifiers, **5**, **26**, **29**, **32**, **36**, **40**, 113, 114, **122**, **124**, 163
Morph, **44**, **131**
Move, 30, **42**, **45**, **64**, 66, 67, **70**, 81, 82, **84**, **91**, 137

N

NanoMesh, **4**, **5**, 62, **63**, **75**, **98**, **100**
New Folder, **69**
NewLight, **143**
Noise, 115, **116**, 158
Normalize Option, **60**
Note, 19, **21**, **47**, 50, **52**, 64, **85**, 86, **91**, **116**, 132, **133**, 134,
  170
Nudge, **45**

O

Offline Activation, **15**
Offset, **64**, **66**, **67**
Online Activation, **14**
Opacity, **120**, **144**

P

Palette Popup, **20**
palettes, **4**, **17**, 19, 20, 23, **54**, 109
Palettes, **19**, **24**
Paste, **53**, 66, **114**, 137
Paste Tool, **53**
PasteMat, **5**, **112**
PasteSH, **114**
Pen, 4, **8**, **9**, 34, **35**
Pen brushes, **4**, **34**
PenA, **34**
PenB, **34**
PenDots, **34**
PenFur, **34**
PenShadow, **34**
PenShadowSilver, **34**
PenShadowSoft, **34**
PenSketch, **34**
PenSoft, **34**
PenWet, **35**
PenWetDots, **35**
PenWetSolid, **35**
Pinch, **43**, **44**
Pivot, **67**
Pixol, **1**, 58, **60**
Planar, 31, **32**
Point, **144**
Polish, 31, 32, **77**, **95**
Polish brushes, **32**
Polish Brushes, **31**

Polygon Ratio, **58**, **60**
Polygroups, **76**, **132**, **133**
PolyGrp, **77**
Polymesh3D, **53**, **73**, **101**
PolyMesh3D, **53**
Polypainting, **34**, **130**, **133**
Presets, **63**
Preview, **55**, **88**, 89, **92**, **112**, 142, **148**, 149, **151**, **154**, **157**,
  162, 163
Project, **18**, 21, **22**, **77**, **95**
Projection Master, 57, **58**, **59**, **60**, **61**
ProjectionShell, **78**
Protect, **5**, **133**, 134, **135**
PushPull, **41**

Q

Quick Select, **121**
QuickSave, **18**, **22**

R

Radial, **47**, **51**, **103**, **107**, **145**
Radius, **40**, 113, **140**, **146**, **152**, **163**
Rays, **146**, **155**
Recalc, **170**
Redshift, **2**, 3, **8**, **9**
Reflectivity, **115**, **116**
Refract, **154**
Remesh, 76, **77**, **100**, **107**
Render Palette, **148**
Render Properties, **112**, **151**, 153, **159**, **163**
Rendering, **6**
Repeat, **66**, 68, **88**
Res, **77**, **155**, 156, **157**
Reset, **65**
Resolution, **55**, **77**, **82**, 92, **94**, **95**, 102, **107**, **170**
Rotate, **64**, 67, **91**, **120**
Run Simulation, **171**

S

Sat, **160**
Saturation, **127**, **128**, **143**, **160**
Scale, **18**, **64**, **67**, 81, **89**, **120**
Scene, **150**, **164**, **165**
Sculpting Brushes, **4**, **25**
SCULPTING BRUSHES, **25**
sculpting tool, **1**
SDiv slider, **55**
See-through, **18**
Self-Collision, **168**

Self-Evaluation Test, **24, 45, 68, 80, 93, 100, 108, 117, 131, 138, 147, 166, 171**
Shadow, **34, 145, 146, 153, 155, 158**
ShadowBox, **5, 100, 101, 102, 103, 104, 105, 106, 107**
Shell, **78, 96**
Shelves, **21**
Shift pressed, **123**
Show Used, **112**
Skinning, **85, 86**
Slope, **163**
Smooth Brush Modes, **26**
Smooth brushes, **25, 26, 27, 29, 86, 136, 137**
Smooth Brushes, **25**
Smudge, **126**
Snake hook, **45**
SnapShot, **123**
Snapshot 3D, **123**
Spec, **113**
Specular, **113, 115, 147, 151**
Split, **74, 79**
Spotlight, **5, 111, 119, 120, 122, 125, 126, 127, 129, 130**
SSS, **112, 113, 157, 159, 163**
Standard, **5, 23, 42, 109, 117**
Startup, **112**
Strength, **32, 36, 113, 154, 155, 156, 158, 163, 167, 169, 171**
Subpalette, **19, 69**
Sub-tool, **54**
Subtools, **55, 68, 77, 88, 99, 103, 116, 157**
SubTools, **4, 54, 55, 68, 69, 71, 72, 73, 74, 75, 76, 77, 103, 123, 132, 153, 170**
Sun, **139, 144**
Symmetry, **3, 47, 48, 49, 50, 51, 103, 107, 132, 133**
System Requirements, **7, 8, 9**

T

Temperature, **113, 164**
Texture Palette, **119**
Texturing, **5, 60, 129**
Tile Proportional, **121**
Tile Selected, **121**
Tile Unified, **121**
Tile V, **125**
Tilt, **142**

Tool, **21, 22, 36, 37, 49, 53, 54, 56, 63, 64, 73, 75, 83, 85, 86, 87, 88, 89, 90, 91, 92, 98, 101, 102, 104, 105, 106, 110, 111, 117, 119, 131, 133, 137, 138, 152, 153, 169**
Tool Palette, **53, 88, 90**
Transform, **47, 48, 49, 50, 51, 65, 102, 103, 107**
Transparency, **82, 103, 115, 154**
TransPose, **64, 66, 67, 78**
Trays, **20, 24**
Trim, **31, 32**

U

Union, **76, 122, 123**
UV Master, **5, 132, 133, 134, 135, 137, 138**
UV MASTER, **132**
UV Seams, **133**

V

VDepth, **156**

W

WaxModfiers, **112**
Weight Strength, **26, 27**

Z

ZBrush, **1, 2, 3, 4, 5, 6, 7, 8, 9, 11, 12, 13, 14, 15, 16, 17, 18, 19, 21, 22, 23, 24, 25, 27, 28, 35, 36, 38, 39, 41, 42, 45, 48, 50, 52, 53, 57, 58, 59, 60, 61, 62, 64, 67, 68, 72, 73, 75, 78, 79, 80, 81, 86, 88, 89, 90, 91, 93, 94, 95, 98, 101, 102, 103, 105, 106, 107, 109, 110, 111, 112, 116, 118, 119, 121, 129, 131, 136, 137, 138, 145, 148, 149, 150, 151, 152, 155, 156, 157, 158, 160, 162, 165, 167, 168, 169, 172**
ZBRUSH, **1, 6, 109, 118**
ZMode, **145, 146**
ZPlugin, **17, 131, 165, 166**
ZRemesher, **2, 4, 5, 97, 98, 100**
ZRemesher 4.0, **2**
ZSketch brushes, **4, 39**
ZSpheres, **4, 39, 40, 41, 81, 82, 83, 84, 85, 86, 87, 88, 90, 91, 133**